Applying Decision Support Systems in Higher Education

John Rohrbaugh, Anne Taylor McCartt, *Editors*

NEW DIRECTIONS FOR INSTITUTIONAL RESEARCH

PATRICK T. TERENZINI, *Editor-in-Chief*
MARVIN W. PETERSON, *Associate Editor*

Number 49, March 1986

Paperback sourcebooks in
The Jossey-Bass Higher Education Series

Jossey-Bass Inc., Publishers
San Francisco • London

John Rohrbaugh, Anne Taylor McCartt (Eds.).
Applying Decision Support Systems in Higher Education.
New Directions for Institutional Research, no. 49.
Volume XIII, Number 1.
San Francisco: Jossey-Bass, 1986.

New Directions for Institutional Research
Patrick T. Terenzini, *Editor-in-Chief*
Marvin W. Peterson, *Associate Editor*

New Directions for Institutional Research (publication number USPS 098-830) is published quarterly by Jossey-Bass Inc., Publishers, and is sponsored by the Association for Institutional Research. The volume and issue numbers above are included for the convenience of libraries. Second-class postage rates are paid at San Francisco, California, and at additional mailing offices.

Correspondence:
Subscriptions, single-issue orders, change of address notices, undelivered copies, and other correspondence should be sent to Subscriptions, Jossey-Bass Inc., Publishers, 433 California Street, San Francisco, California 94104.

Editorial correspondence should be sent to the Editor-in-Chief, Patrick T. Terenzini, Office of Institutional Research, SUNY, Albany, New York 12222.

Library of Congress Catalog Card Number 85-81890

International Standard Serial Number ISSN 0271-0579

International Standard Book Number ISBN 87589-719-3

Cover art by WILLI BAUM

Manufactured in the United States of America

Ordering Information

The paperback sourcebooks listed below are published quarterly and can be ordered either by subscription or single-copy.

Subscriptions cost $40.00 per year for institutions, agencies, and libraries. Individuals can subscribe at the special rate of $30.00 per year *if payment is by personal check.* (Note that the full rate of $40.00 applies if payment is by institutional check, even if the subscription is designated for an individual.) Standing orders are accepted.

Single copies are available at $9.95 when payment accompanies order, and *all single-copy orders under $25.00 must include payment.* (California, New Jersey, New York, and Washington, D.C., residents please include appropriate sales tax.) For billed orders, cost per copy is $9.95 plus postage and handling. (Prices subject to change without notice.)

Bulk orders (ten or more copies) of any individual sourcebook are available at the following discounted prices: 10–49 copies, $8.95 each; 50–100 copies, $7.96 each; over 100 copies, *inquire.* Sales tax and postage and handling charges apply as for single copy orders.

To ensure correct and prompt delivery, all orders must give either the *name of an individual* or an *official purchase order number.* Please submit your order as follows:

Subscriptions: specify series and year subscription is to begin.
Single Copies: specify sourcebook code (such as, IR1) and first two words of title.

Mail orders for United States and Possessions, Latin America, Canada, Japan, Australia, and New Zealand to:
Jossey-Bass Inc., Publishers
433 California Street
San Francisco, California 94104

Mail orders for all other parts of the world to:
Jossey-Bass Limited
28 Banner Street
London EC1Y 8QE

New Directions for Institutional Research Series
Patrick T. Terenzini, *Editor-in-Chief*
Marvin W. Peterson, *Associate Editor*

IR1 *Evaluating Institutions for Accountability,* Howard R. Bowen
IR2 *Assessing Faculty Effort,* James I. Doi
IR3 *Toward Affirmative Action,* Lucy W. Sells
IR4 *Organizing Nontraditional Study,* Samuel Baskin

IR5 *Evaluating Statewide Boards,* Robert O. Berdahl
IR6 *Assuring Academic Progress Without Growth,* Allan M. Cartter
IR7 *Responding to Changing Human Resource Needs,* Raul Heist, Jonathan R. Warren
IR8 *Measuring and Increasing Academic Productivity,* Robert A. Wallhaus
IR9 *Assessing Computer-Based System Models,* Thomas R. Mason
IR10 *Examining Departmental Management,* James Smart, James Montgomery
IR11 *Allocating Resources Among Departments,* Paul L. Dressel, Lou Anna Kimsey Simon
IR12 *Benefiting from Interinstitutional Research,* Marvin W. Peterson
IR13 *Applying Analytic Methods to Planning and Management,* David S. P. Hopkins, Roger G. Scroeder
IR14 *Protecting Individual Rights to Privacy in Higher Education,* Alton L. Taylor
IR15 *Appraising Information Needs of Decision Makers,* Carl R. Adams
IR16 *Increasing the Public Accountability of Higher Education,* John K. Folger
IR17 *Analyzing and Constructing Cost,* Meredith A. Gonyea
IR18 *Employing Part-Time Faculty,* David W. Leslie
IR19 *Using Goals in Research and Planning,* Robert Fenske
IR20 *Evaluting Faculty Performance and Vitality,* Wayne C. Kirschling
IR21 *Developing a Total Marketing Plan,* John A. Lucas
IR22 *Examining New Trends in Administrative Computing,* E. Michael Staman
IR23 *Professional Development for Institutional Research,* Robert G. Cope
IR24 *Planning Rational Retrenchment,* Alfred L. Cooke
IR25 *The Impact of Student Financial Aid on Institutions,* Joe B. Henry
IR26 *The Autonomy of Public Colleges,* Paul L. Dressel
IR27 *Academic Program Evaluation,* Eugene C. Craven
IR28 *Academic Planning for the 1980s,* Richard B. Heydinger
IR29 *Institutional Assessment for Self-Improvement,* Richard I. Miller
IR30 *Coping with Faculty Reduction,* Stephen R. Hample
IR31 *Evaluation of Management and Planning Systems,* Nick L. Poulton
IR32 *Increasing the Use of Program Evaluation,* Jack Lindquist
IR33 *Effective Planned Change Strategies,* G. Melvin Hipps
IR34 *Qualitative Methods for Institutional Research,* Eileen Kuhns, S. V. Martorana
IR35 *Information Technology: Advances and Applications,* Bernard Sheehan
IR36 *Studying Student Attrition,* Ernest T. Pascarella
IR37 *Using Research for Strategic Planning,* Norman P. Uhl
IR38 *The Politics and Pragmatics of Institutional Research,* James W. Firnberg, William F. Lasher
IR39 *Applying Methods and Techniques of Futures Research,* James L. Morrison, William L. Renfro, Wayne I. Boucher
IR40 *College Faculty: Versatile Human Resources in a Period of Constraint,* Roger G. Baldwin, Robert T. Blackburn
IR41 *Determining the Effectiveness of Campus Services,* Robert A. Scott
IR42 *Issues in Pricing Undergraduate Education,* Larry H. Litten
IR43 *Responding to New Realities in Funding,* Larry L. Leslie
IR44 *Using Microcomputers for Planning and Management Support,* William L. Tetlow
IR45 *Impact and Challenges of a Changing Federal Role,* Virginia Ann Hodgkinson
IR46 *Institutional Research in Transition,* Marvin W. Peterson, Mary Corcoran

IR47 *Assessing Educational Outcomes,* Peter T. Ewell
IR48 *The Use of Data in Discrimination Issues Cases,* William Rosenthal, Bernard Yancey

Contents

The Association for Institutional Research was created in 1966 to benefit, assist, and advance research leading to improved understanding, planning, and operation of institutions of higher education. Publication policy is set by its Publications Board.

For information about the Association for Institutional Research, write:

AIR Executive Office
314 Stone Building
Florida State University
Tallahassee, FL 32306

(904) 644-4470

Editors' Notes

This sourcebook offers an introduction to the application of Decision Support Systems (DSS) in institutional settings. It is edited to be instructive and useful to those institutional researchers for whom DSS may be a new concept and to any individual with responsibility for improving decision-making processes in an organization. A variety of decision models and problem types have been selected to illustrate the range of practical functions that DSS can be designed to serve.

The organization of this sourcebook has been planned to build interest in DSS, as well as to facilitate learning. Following a brief introduction, the text is divided into two major sections that explore the uses of DSS for tactical and strategic decisions. Overviews provide background information and perspective on both types of applications. Two illustrative chapters offer concise examples in institutional settings. In each example, a different decision model and problem type is explored.

In Chapter One, Rohrbaugh introduces the application of DSS in higher education by defining the key issues and offering historical perspective. It is argued that institutional research supports decision making in higher education and that the profession should take a leadership role in the design and implementation of DSS within institutions.

Chapter Two provides the overview for the first section which is devoted to DSS applications for tactical decision making. Harmon discusses how the development of comprehensive, systematic, and explicit sets of procedures for repetitive decisions enables DSS to reduce the amount of institutional resources invested in the continual reconstruction of tactical decision processes.

The first extended illustration of tactical decision support is provided by Feldt in Chapter Three. Markov chains (one type of probability model developed through operations research) are used to project periodic changes in the likely composition of units. In this instance, tactical workforce planning is the activity supported by DSS.

McCartt suggests in Chapter Four that tenure cases be represented as tactical decisions. She proposes DSS development based on a multiattribute utility model, so that the uniqueness and complexity of each case do not overshadow the need for institutional accountability. Explicit sets of procedures for systematically integrating comprehensive information about individual performance are described.

Chapter Five provides the overview for the second section, which deals with DSS applications for strategic decision making. McGrath argues that, since an institution's nonroutine decisions cannot be preformulated, model building for strategic decision making can be made more effective by developing Group Decision Support Systems (GDSS) to deal with truly novel and complex problems.

In Chapter Six, Milter illustrates the use of GDSS for institution-wide allocations of organizational resources among competing claims of priority. He examines a benefit-cost approach to such strategic decisions; a model of resource allocation is constructed by the executive team of a university to guide the distribution of its discretionary budget.

The use of system dynamics models in strategic decision making is illustrated by Chen in Chapter Seven. She describes how such models allow decision makers to anticipate cause-and-effect relationships and, by simulating the future in a comprehensive manner, to create a GDSS for synthetic trial-and-error testing of alternative courses of action with respect to institutional pricing.

The final chapter surveys problems of DSS and GDSS design, implementation, and evaluation. Rohrbaugh places particular emphasis on the fact that DSS and GDSS need not be extensive and expensive to be effective. Institutional development can be initiated on a small and manageable scale.

Our intention in editing this sourcebook has been to incorporate a diversity of issues that affect successful applications of DSS in higher education. No one theme will be found to dominate discussion. Fair treatment is given to the problems of facilitating organizational change, of selecting computer software, of securing administrative participation, and of structuring a mathematical model. It is our hope that this sourcebook will enable the profession of institutional research to adopt a more holistic view of decision support than has been achieved in other organizational settings.

John Rohrbaugh
Anne Taylor McCartt
Editors

John Rohrbaugh is associate professor in the Rockefeller College of Public Affairs and Policy, State University of New York at Albany.

Anne Taylor McCartt is program manager with the Institute for Traffic Safety Management and Research, Rockefeller College of Public Affairs and Policy, State University of New York at Albany.

Part 1.

Introduction

The advent of Decision Support Systems redefines the primary professional role for institutional researchers.

Institutional Research as Decision Support

John Rohrbaugh

The Definition of Decision Support Systems

Any system that supports a decision is a decision support system. The focus of this sourcebook, however, is on Decision Support Systems (DSS) as interactive computer-based sets of procedures that assist decision makers in using information to analyze possible implications and contingencies of alternative courses of action. A closer examination of this definition is essential to clarify the intended focus.

Interactive Computer-Based. Although a pen, calendar, and notepad may well serve as a decision support system, the type of DSS considered here depends primarily on the use of a computer. Whether mainframe, minicomputer, or microcomputer, the computer must be capable of receiving requests directly from decision makers and reporting directly to them.

Sets of Procedures. Specific DSS applications are created with the use of software, that is, instructions to the computer that are programmed in one of many special-purpose or higher-level languages (for example, PASCAL, APL, or BASIC). The computer programs which comprise DSS can be written to produce a wide variety of extensive and complex analyses with sophisticated graphics displays. Each application is tailored to specific decision settings.

J. Rohrbaugh, A. T. McCartt (Eds.). *Applying Decision Support Systems in Higher Education.* New Directions for Institutional Research, no. 49. San Francisco: Jossey-Bass, March 1986.

That Assist Decision Makers. DSS are not developed to make decisions or replace the current decision makers but rather to support and enhance decision makers' efforts at exercising their own best judgment. Although many descriptions of DSS have focused on corporate uses for senior management functions, DSS could serve as an adjunct to any and all decision makers.

In Using Information. Many of the early DSS applications (with notable exceptions) were inextricably tied to the primary use of information that had already been machine-coded and stored in automated files. Because most decision making relies at least as much on "soft" data (such as opinions, beliefs, judgments, attitudes, and values) as on computerized record keeping, DSS are increasingly designed to incorporate a wide range of information sources, from objective "facts" to subjective "best guesses."

To Analyze. To improve the effectiveness (rather than just the efficiency) of decision making, DSS make available a broad array of analytical techniques to guide thorough investigations of problems. DSS applications have incorporated not only standard statistical routines but also alternative approaches, including simultaneous equations, probability models, formal logic, and set theory.

Possible Implications and Contingencies. DSS design makes it possible to ask various types of "what if" questions—an essential part of the process of making good decisions. For example, intended and unintended consequences of a decision can be anticipated in a variety of future scenarios, sensitivity analyses can be conducted to test whether certain assessments are critical to the decision process, and repeated projections can be produced to forecast "who gets what" as conditions change.

Of Alternative Courses of Action. Ultimately, DSS assist decision makers in their identification of and commitment to preferred alternative courses of action (variously described as options, policies, choices, candidates, or strategies). DSS can even help in making decisions not to decide ("no-decision decisions"), whether they are made explicitly, implicitly, or by default.

The Origin of Decision Support Systems

The origin of DSS can be traced to two major programs of study: the theoretical work on organizational decision making conducted primarily at the Carnegie Institute of Technology (March and Simon, 1958; Simon, 1960; Cyert and March, 1963); and the technical work on time-shared processing systems conducted primarily at the Massachusetts Institute of Technology (Greenberger, 1962; Corbato, 1963; McCarthy and others, 1963). By 1970, there were published reports about the first applications of this advanced computer processing to address the problems of management.

The descriptions of projects in the early years of DSS revealed optimism that the newly developed technology could be appropriately (but not always easily) adapted to provide highly practical aids for enhancing the process of reaching organizational decisions. Little (1970) offered a set of rigorous standards for the young field: Its computer-based procedures should be readily understandable, resilient to mistakes that users might make, easy to adjust and control, flexible enough to be readily modified and updated, inclusive of all important elements of the decision (including subjective estimates), and, of course, efficient to use. Scott Morton (1971) is credited with implementing one of the first such systems to support production planning and decision making; it was an effort consciously guided by concerns about the organizational context of implementation as well as the features of the technology itself. He also proposed a phrase to describe his integrative approach: *management decision systems.* Gerrity (1971) soon followed Scott Morton's approach with the design of a much more extensive system to support investment management. Over the next few years, more than fifty major, organization-wide applications of DSS (as they now had become known) were identified (Alter, 1977), and the first books devoted to DSS appeared (Keen and Scott Morton, 1978; McCosh and Scott Morton, 1978).

Technical Development. The technical effort devoted to developing DSS has been remarkably eclectic, resulting in a blurring of its boundaries with such interrelated fields as systems engineering (Savitzky, 1985; Paker, 1983), data processing management (Thierauf, 1984; Mader, 1979), operations research (Levin and others, 1986; Eppen and Gould, 1984), and artificial intelligence (Haugeland, 1985; Hayes-Roth and others, 1983). During the same period of time, these fields have broadened their own interest in the practical problems of implementation, resulting in adaptations of their technologies for improved decision support. As a result, advances in DSS are often nearly indistinguishable from certain accomplishments in the constituent fields.

The relationship of DSS to the field of systems engineering is a significant example. Although improvements in hardware and software, such as real-time processing, time-sharing, and multiprogramming, led to the construction of very large and centralized computer systems (in a promising but ill-fated quest to produce completely integrated databases—"total systems"), they simultaneously made possible very small and decentralized subsystems, in which DSS applications with circumscribed information needs could thrive. The availability of ever more inexpensive but powerful minicomputers and microcomputers (with options for graphic displays in full color) has profoundly accelerated the trend toward personalized computing. Meanwhile, a steady evolution in software has markedly improved the ease of programming and the versatility of programs. There is even a variety of specialized software packages, called "generators," marketed to facilitate the construction of specific DSS.

Other innovations in systems engineering, such as random access memory, magnetic disks, and mass-storage systems, were directed more at increasing the efficiency of the clerical operations that electronic data processing (EDP) had traditionally supported (for example, automating payroll, invoicing, inventory, and personnel records) than at increasing the effectiveness of organizational decision making. However, the expansion of EDP management to include systems designed to facilitate all facets of an organization's information collection, storage, and retrieval placed entirely new demands on hardware and software development. Subsequent advances in technology permitted not only the generation of automated reports at regular intervals but also immediate access to all of an organization's automated files. Management information systems (MIS) began to be designed to enhance such direct access, so that the records most suited to managers' information needs might be readily available in a useful form. Because effective decision making depends in part upon an adequate knowledge of past and present conditions (which may require substantial amounts of data processing to summarize appropriately), the development of sophisticated MIS tools has made a significant contribution to state-of-the-art DSS.

Nevertheless, decision making demands more than mere access to information. Although the technology of MIS can provide efficient answers to fundamental "what is" questions, effective choices among alternative courses of action also require explicit consideration of future implications and contingencies—answers to "what if" questions. For this reason, the field of operations research (OR) and management science (MS), established over 20 years before the advent of DSS, has been devoted primarily to the building of mathematical models (most prominently simulation and optimization models). These models are used to solve many of the operation and control problems of management, such as transporting, scheduling, financing, and marketing. Although the belief was that complex problems could be subjected to analytic models that would produce better outcomes for organizations than continued reliance on certain decision makers, actual implementation efforts frequently failed. Not surprisingly, the beginning of developmental work on DSS coincided with a growing pragmatic concern in the OR/MS field with the applied problems of mathematical modeling for client organizations.

In contrast to OR/MS, which is typified by the use of formal mathematical theory as the basis of model building, the field of artificial intelligence (AI), particularly in its constituent area of problem solving, has developed heuristic model building based on an individual's knowledge, judgment, and experience to produce computer-based expert systems (ES). ES attempt not only to make implicit cognitive processes more explicit but also to specify synthetic rules ("inference engines") that in practice would lead to identical conclusions (for example, correctly diagnosing a disease or locating a rich mineral deposit). Although users of ES can question inferences and examine the underlying lines of reasoning to build their confidence in the answer provided, they do not modify any of the elements of the model itself; the intent is to duplicate indisputable expertise. It would appear that this reification of "single-minded right thinking" would be inconsistent with the consultative ethic underlying most DSS applications. Nevertheless, an important contribution of the work on ES (in the broadest definition of the field) has been the demonstration that heuristic structures based on "soft" data, typically not available in computer-based information systems, can play an important role in the design of systems for decision support.

The Use of Sociopsychological Research. Technical advances aside, there is little in the DSS literature over the past fifteen years to indicate sustained interest in ongoing sociopsychological research pertinent to organizational decision making. As constructive criticism, Bahl and Hunt (1985) reemphasized "an elementary point that is often overlooked in practice, namely, that designing an effective decision support system is a complex, cognitively guided, problem solving task that can only be done well in close collaboration with the system's user. . . . Design attention needs to concentrate on decision makers rather than on decisions" (p. 87). The problem, of course, is that the study of decision makers in organizational settings has been less the focus of EDP, MIS, OR/MS, AI, or ES than of behavioral decision theory (Kahneman and others, 1982; Pitz and Sachs, 1984; Hammond and Arkes, 1986), organization development (Kimberly and Quinn, 1984; Kanter, 1983; Tichy, 1983), group dynamics (McGrath, 1984; Guzzo, 1982; Brandstatter and others, 1982), and organizational behavior (Schein, 1985; Kilman, 1985; Pfeffer, 1981). Yet the technical work on DSS is almost as distant from these fields of study as it was in 1970.

There is little doubt, however, that major advances in DSS applications will be achieved only with greater understanding of decision-making behaviors at the individual, group, and organizational levels. At the individual level, for example, research in behavioral decision theory has pointed to a variety of problems characteristic of cognitive functioning that must be addressed if DSS are ever to offer effective remedies. The growing literature on behavioral decision theory has underscored the extraordinary care that must be taken to overcome the subtle biases and implicit limitations reflected in most cognitive processes. At the group level, research devoted to the study of organizational units, management teams, and committee meetings has led to improved methods for facilitating collective decision making. As a result, recent discussion of the need for group decision support systems has emphasized the critical importance of the field of group dynamics to the technical work on decision support.

In designing DSS, it should be impossible to ignore related developments occurring in the fields of organizational behavior and organizational development. It is obvious that DSS induce change in organizations. Not only do they change the ways in which organizational problems are defined and solved; they also frequently affect communication patterns, power relations, reward structures, and, occasionally, the entire organizational culture. DSS are not merely installed by technicians in static and neutral institutional environments. DSS designers are agents of organizational change. The potential impact of DSS on institutions (including the resistance to change that may be generated) indicates a significant need for more comprehensive understanding of organizational behavior and organizational development. As yet, the cumulative literature of these fields has not been well integrated with proposals for appropriate DSS design and implementation.

Decision Support as an Adaptive Process

Rather than emphasizing the technical features of a DSS application as a *finished product,* that is, as an idealized set of computer-based procedures that entirely fulfills decision makers' needs, at least some attention is being directed at the evolutionary development of decision support as a *continuing service.* In Keen's (1980) view, for example, the definition of DSS should not focus on any "final" system but on the continuous learning about a DSS application that is required of both its users and its designers. Only over an extended period of time can designers fully understand what particular decision makers need or are likely to use. Similarly, decision makers do not always know immediately what they want or what can be designed to support them. Decision situations are shaped by the availability of specific DSS that often evoke new insights from designers and users alike. As a result, decision support may be better represented as an incremental, adaptive process than as a completed project.

Many DSS applications have a rather narrow initial scope, offering only a few advantages over unaided decision making. Designers have not hesitated to begin their work in an organization with "elementary," "first-cut," or "trial-and-error" approaches to DSS implementation. Because these systems are known to evolve, the key has been to provide at least a modicum of decision support that would be flexible enough to permit incremental modifications and extensions. Actual uses of DSS over time are reported to diverge markedly from those originally planned. Individual decision makers may take advantage of different features of the same system, simultaneously pushing enhancements in a variety of directions. In fact, user participation in all developmental phases of decision support is considered a hallmark of good design.

If decision support depends upon an adaptive and participatory process of system development, designers must fulfill social as well as technical responsibilities. For example, attracting and maintaining decision makers' involvement is often a challenging task. Assuring that subsequent stages of system development remain responsive to decision makers' changing needs (both expressed and inferred) demands relentless effort. Educating decision makers about new possibilities for more effective decision support in an area that already seems to be well-structured (or introducing an innovative idea for decision support in an unstructured problem area) requires a balance of personal enthusiasm and organizational realism.

The Role of Institutional Research as Decision Support

The contemporary literature on DSS (Alter, 1980; Bonzcek and others, 1981; Sprague and Carlson, 1982; Thierauf, 1982; Bennett, 1983) should speak directly to institutional researchers who view their role as collecting, analyzing, and preparing information for university decision makers. Responsibility for decision support entails much more than providing the capacity to pose and answer "what is" questions, no matter how important such questions may be. Although a greater volume of data can be made rapidly available through ever more flexible and efficient MIS technology, what administrators need most is greater support in integrating information, beliefs, and values. After all available data have been retrieved, organized, and summarized, there is still a need for systematic decision-making assistance that accommodates subjective considerations—methods that allow not only for analysis but also for the political drama of negotiation, bargaining, compromise, and consensus building. Development of DSS has responded to Ackoff's (1967) often-cited assertion that the weaknesses in decision processes stem primarily from the inadequacy of the structures unwittingly imposed on available information rather than from any lack of information per se.

Most institutions already have the technology to develop interactive computer-based sets of procedures to assist decision makers in using information to analyze possible implications and contingencies of alternative courses of action. What most institutions lack, however, are individuals charged with the responsibility of beginning the adaptive and incremental process of DSS development. Rather than viewing institutional researchers as mere intermediaries who must protect naive decision makers from the flawed but finished products of DSS technicians (see Sheehan, 1984), one well might argue that institutional researchers should assume full responsibility for initiating DSS applications.

The relationship between DSS designers and users must be direct and personal in order to assure adaptive development. Because DSS may be considered services rather than products, the work of incremental design is much more than a job for a technician. Furthermore, the close collaboration necessary between designers and users in developing DSS, to assure that appropriate enhancements will occur, strongly militates against any "intermediary" role. The purpose of this sourcebook is to suggest ways in which institutional research might become synonymous with the design and development of adaptive processes for decision support. As Joel Harmon concludes in Chapter Two, it is a role that institutional researchers are well suited and well positioned to play.

References

Ackoff, R. L. "Management Misinformation Systems." *Management Science,* 1967, *14,* B147–B156.

Alter, S. L. "A Taxonomy of Decision Support Systems." *Sloan Management Review,* 1977, *19,* 39–56.

Alter, S. L. *Decision Support Systems: Current Practice and Continuing Challenges.* Reading, Mass.: Addison-Wesley, 1980.

Bahl, H. C., and Hunt, R. G. "Problem-solving Strategies for DSS Design." *Information and Management,* 1985, *8,* 81–88.

Bennett, J. L. *Building Decision Support Systems.* Reading, Mass.: Addison-Wesley, 1983.

Bonzcek, R. H., Holsapple, C. W., and Whinston, A. B. *Foundations of Decision Support Systems.* New York: Academic Press, 1981.

Brandstatter, H., Davis, J. H., and Stocker-Kreichgauer, G. (Eds.). *Group Decision Making.* New York: Academic Press, 1982.

Corbato, F. J. *The Compatible Time-Sharing System—A Programmer's Guide.* Boston: M.I.T. Press, 1963.

Cyert, R. M., and March, J. G. *A Behavioral Theory of the Firm.* Englewood Cliffs, N.J.: Prentice-Hall, 1963.

Eppen, G. D., and Gould, F. J. *Introductory Management Science.* Englewood Cliffs, N. J.: Prentice-Hall, 1984.

Gerrity, T. P., Jr. "The Design of Man-Machine Decision Systems: An Application to Portfolio Management." *Sloan Management Review,* 1971, *12,* 59–75.

Greenberger, M. (Ed.). *Management and the Computer of the Future.* Boston: M.I.T. Press, 1962.

Guzzo, R. A. (Ed.). *Improving Decision Making in Organizations: Approaches from Theory and Research.* New York: Academic Press, 1982.

Hammond, K. R., and Arkes, H. (Eds.). *Judgment and Decision Making: An Interdisciplinary Reader.* New York: Cambridge University Press, 1986.

Haugeland, J. *Artificial Intelligence: The Very Idea.* Boston: M.I.T. Press, 1985.

Hayes-Roth, F., Waterman, D. A., and Lenat, D. B. (Eds.). *Building Expert Systems.* Reading, Mass.: Addison-Wesley, 1983.

Kahneman, D., Slovic, P., and Tversky, A. (Eds.). *Judgment under Uncertainty: Heuristics and Biases.* New York: Cambridge University Press, 1982.

Kanter, R. M. *The Change Masters: Innovations for Productivity in the American Corporation.* New York: Simon & Schuster, 1983.

Keen, P. G. W. "Adaptive Design for DSS." *Data Base,* 1980, *12,* 15–25.

Keen, P. G. W., and Scott Morton, M. S. *Decision Support Systems: An Organizational Perspective.* Reading, Mass.: Addison-Wesley, 1978.

Kilman, R. H. *Beyond the Quick Fix.* San Francisco, Jossey-Bass, 1985.

Kimberly, J. R., and Quinn, R. E. (Eds.). *New Futures: The Challenge of Managing Corporate Transitions.* Homewood, Ill.: Dow Jones-Irwin, 1984.

Levin, R. I., Rubin, D. S., and Stinson, J. P. *Quantitative Approaches to Management.* New York: McGraw-Hill, 1986.

Little, J. D. C. "Models and Managers: The Concept of a Decision Calculus." *Management Science,* 1970, *16,* B466–B485.

McCarthy, J., Boilen, S., Fredkin, E., and Licklider, J. C. R. "A Time-Sharing Debugging System for a Small Computer." *AFIPS Conference Proceedings,* 1963, *23,* 51–58.

McCosh, A. M., and Scott Morton, M. S. *Management Decision Support Systems.* London: Macmillan, 1978.

McGrath, J. E. *Groups: Interaction and Performance.* Englewood Cliffs, N.J.: Prentice-Hall, 1984.

Mader, C. *Information Systems: Technology, Economics, Applications.* Chicago: Science Research Associates, 1979.

March, J. G., and Simon, H. A. *Organizations.* New York: Wiley, 1958.

Paker, Y. *Multi-Microprocessor Systems.* New York: Academic Press, 1983.

Pfeffer, J. *Power in Organizations.* Boston: Pitman, 1981.

Pitz, G. F., and Sachs, N. J. "Judgment and Decision: Theory and Application." In M. R. Rosenzweig and L. W. Porter (Eds.), *Annual Review of Psychology.* Palo Alto, Calif.: Annual Reviews, 1984.

Savitzky, S. R. *Real-Time Microprocessor Systems.* New York: Van Nostrand Reinhold, 1985.

Schein, E. H. *Organizational Culture and Leadership.* San Francisco: Jossey-Bass, 1985.

Scott Morton, M. S. *Management Decision Systems.* Boston: Harvard University Press, 1971.

Sheehan, B. S. "Measurement for Decision Support." *Research in Higher Education,* 1984, *20,* 193–210.

Simon, H. A. *The New Science of Management Decision.* New York: Harper & Row, 1960.

Sprague, R. H., Jr., and Carlson, E. D. *Building Effective Decision Support Systems.* Englewood Cliffs, N.J.: Prentice-Hall, 1982.

Thierauf, R. J. *Decision Support Systems for Effective Planning and Control.* Englewood Cliffs, N.J.: Prentice-Hall, 1982.

Thierauf, R. J. *Effective Management Information Systems.* Columbus, Ohio: Charles Merrill, 1984.

Tichy, N. M. *Managing Strategic Change.* New York: Wiley, 1983.

John Rohrbaugh is associate professor in the Rockefeller College of Public Affairs and Policy, State University of New York at Albany.

Part 2.

Tactical Decision Support

Even with their potential barely tapped, DSS are making significant contributions to improving decision-making effectiveness in institutions.

Tactical Decision Making and Decision Support Systems

Joel I. Harmon

Microcomputer technology is everywhere in instititutions of higher education today, and this is not surprising. As the number of "bits for the buck" continues to rise dramatically and the pace of software development accelerates, microcomputers are becoming increasingly affordable, powerful, and friendly. Almost every educational unit laments its "under-computerization," and vendors are scrambling to fill the gap, often with promotional arrangements that are quite favorable to the receiving institution. Yet, even as desktop computers are sprouting in the institutional landscape like mushrooms after a rain, experts generally acknowledge that most are being tapped for only a fraction of their true potential (Suttle, 1984; Kling and Scacchi, 1980).

Although microcomputer applications for research work, text processing, and database management are fairly common, most institutional decision makers have hardly begun to capitalize on their much more powerful potential for decision support and telecommunication. In those cases where decision support systems (DSS) are being used to full advantage, evidence is mounting that the effectiveness of institutional decision making is improving. This chapter will examine some of those cases and, to some extent, the reasons why there are not yet more of them.

The particular focus here is on tactical decision making and the

J. Rohrbaugh, A. T. McCartt (Eds.). *Applying Decision Support Systems in Higher Education.*
New Directions for Institutional Research, no. 49. San Francisco: Jossey-Bass, March 1986.

potential advantages of DSS in tactical situations. Some of the types of tactical institutional decisions for which DSS are being used are reviewed, with particular emphasis on the advantages observed and the problems encountered. The chapter concludes with a brief examination of the future of DSS, particularly those issues that many feel need to be addressed in order to integrate DSS more fully into the tactical decision-making processes of an institution.

Why DSS Are Needed for Tactical Problems—A Scenario

For the past two years Elaine Simpson has been in charge of the Office of Space Utilization of a metropolitan university. Like many institutions, the university has experienced considerable internal and external pressure for the efficient use of space. Accordingly, Ms. Simpson is often required to evaluate past space utilization patterns, assess current and projected availability, and make recommendations regarding specific proposals for changes in space allocation. The demands of this ongoing decision-making process are a source of continuing frustration to her. Given the large network of facilities and programs, the process of identifying, evaluating, and choosing among options is a taxing one. Among the many factors entering into consideration are: program growth rates and shifting programmatic needs; rates of facility obsolescence, modification, and acquisition; constraints of a budgetary and regulatory nature (for example, access for the handicapped) and the implications of space allocation decisions for other facility programs such as operation and maintenance. Further, her recommendations must be consonant with initiatives stated in the university's strategic plan.

Ms. Simpson often feels ill-prepared to consider the many factors, complex relationships, and uncertainties that are involved in the space allocation process. "There is certainly no shortage of data," she acknowledges. "In fact, I'm sometimes overwhelmed by all our reports. The difficult part is converting our printouts into useful information and, even then, so much of our work involves responding to priorities, not to facts. On many occasions I feel that my recommendations would be improved if I could examine more closely some other key issues that usually take a back seat. The problem is that exploratory questions just cause my staff to groan under the weight of additional work required to get more data." She further laments that many of those who are affected by her recommendations "just don't seem to appreciate the constraints of our decision-making process." As pressure for accountability in space allocation mounts, Elaine Simpson continues to muddle through.

This hypothetical scenario could easily be recreated for a large number of other institutional administrators who, at times, also share a feeling of being overwhelmed by the complexity and pressure of their decision-making environments. Hospital and health care administrators struggle with difficult case-mix problems. Library managers are perplexed by both the objective and subjective costs and benefits of various resource-sharing networks. Directors of large research organizations try to balance their "portfolios" of research projects, and various admissions and personnel offices endeavor to create and implement systematic, fair, and effective evaluation procedures. The problems on this short list share a common feature: all require tactical decisions that could benefit from the application of DSS.

What Are Tactical Problems?

For the purposes of discussion here, we can broadly define tactical problems as those that lie toward the middle of a continuum from programmed to nonprogrammed decisions (Simon, 1960). Programmed decisions (for example, much institutional food purchasing or equipment maintenance) are so entirely routine, well-defined, and value-free that they are capable of being objectively analyzed, structured, and completely automated. Ideally, such operational decisions do not require decision makers so much as analysts with techniques to generate optimal solutions. At the other end of the continuum, nonprogrammed or strategic decisions, to borrow Drucker's (1954) phrase, usually involve what Mason and Mitroff (1981) characterized as "wicked problems," those problems that are so unique, ill-defined, and of such major consequence to the entire institution as to be solvable only through a collective and political process involving all of the affected personnel. Tactical decisions are semi-structured and lie in the broad area between these two extremes, involving problems that recur frequently enough that they can be reasonably well anticipated. They are predictable enough to benefit from computer support, but they also require the exercise of considerable judgment and value expression in the process of defining the problem, identifying possible courses of action, and formulating decision rules.

Admittedly, the distinction between tactical and strategic decisions can become fuzzy. Strategic decisions can also benefit from computer support. In fact, the second section of this sourcebook describes the application of group decision support systems to the type of unstructured problems that ten years ago were thought to be inaccessible to DSS (Keen and Scott Morton, 1978). The important differences to be stressed for the purposes of this discussion concern frequency, time frame, and locus of responsibility. Strategic decisions, as we have defined them here, are those made infrequently in response to unique organizational problems of major consequence, whereas a given type of tactical decision is likely to be made more frequently as part of a continuing process of evaluation (and reevaluation). Additionally, tactical decisions typically involve a short-term time

focus, while strategic decisions are made with a view to the long term (typically, three to five years or more). Finally, the responsibility for any one type of tactical decision is more likely to be given to an individual decision maker, while strategic decisions usually involve two or more senior executives.

Donovan and Madnick (1977) distinguished the use of "institutional DSS" for work with tactical problems. Although institutional DSS are tangible products, Keen and Scott Morton (1978) stress that DSS are better thought of as services. They prescribe several key characteristics for a DSS service. First, DSS should permit managers to investigate both the objective and subjective aspects of their problems in an interactive and exploratory manner. Second, DSS should be flexible and customized to the unique nature of each task and should allow information to be processed according to the unique cognitive styles of each decision maker. Third, the entire computer-aided decision-making process should be under the full control of the individual; DSS should not attempt to automate the decision process, predefine objectives, or impose solutions. Not all tactical problems justify using a decision support system. Whether or not a problem is a good candidate for DSS may be judged according to three characteristics: frequency, importance, and information intensity.

Administrators who find themselves repeatedly facing a problem with a fairly consistent structure are well advised to consider the use of DSS. Returning to the scenario presented earlier, the factors that entered into Elaine Simpson's space allocation decisions appeared to be fairly consistent from one semester to the next—various budgetary and operating costs, program needs, and projected space inventories, for example. These recurring aspects of her problem could be identified and structured through DSS. Certainly, she could expect that the state of each issue and its importance to herself and to the organization might change over time, and that intangible concerns would remain difficult to specify. Recall, however, that one of the main reasons why the problem Ms. Simpson faced was a tactical (semi-structured) one, rather than a programmable (structured) one, was that her judgment and insight were absolutely essential. How frequent is frequent enough to justify DSS? Weekly and monthly decisions, and perhaps even yearly ones, are good candidates, depending on other characteristics such as the importance of the problem.

Unless a tactical problem is of some importance to the individual decision maker or the institution, the time and expense of configuring DSS to handle that problem are not likely to be justified. The more important a problem, the less frequently it would need to recur in order to justify DSS. The problem facing Elaine Simpson was obviously an important one because the effectiveness of space allocation decisions has major budgetary, programmatic, and political implications. Because concern for accountability is likely to be high in such situations, there is a strong need to be thorough and explicit in the decision-making process. Thus, institutional administrators facing annual "high stakes" problems can benefit greatly from using DSS.

Problems that are neither very frequent nor extremely important may still warrant use of DSS if they are information-intensive. Information intensity is a function of the size of the database involved and the degree of complexity and uncertainty associated with the problem. Problems that require turning a great deal of data into information are good candidates—for example, course registrations or applications for admissions. Greater complexity and uncertainty increase an administrator's need for information (Galbraith, 1977) and, consequently, the amount of data that need to be processed. The space allocation example is a highly complex one, because a large number of factors are involved and because there exist a number of dynamic relationships between several components of the problem. Further, the process is subject to several uncertainties, such as program growth rates, budget allocations, and institutional priorities. Not surprisingly, Elaine Simpson's need for information was great. Information-intensive problems are likely to consume a good deal of a unit's time in the process of transforming data into information. Recall Ms. Simpson's concern over the burden placed on her staff in order to produce the kind of meaningful information she needed to make sound decisions. As is typical in the absence of DSS, the costs of obtaining appropriate information seemed to be prohibitive.

Even if sufficient high-quality information is made available to administrators, they must still face the taxing process of integrating and evaluating that information in order to make a decision. This may be particularly difficult when complexity and uncertainty are high. It may be difficult for an administrator to handle the trade-offs between the many competing issues involved. Moreover, the problem may become even more difficult when the future is uncertain, because the importance of certain issues may change, as well as their relationships to credible solutions. Elaine Simpson seemed to sense that her need to oversimplify the problem (by omitting certain potentially important considerations) and her inability to explore more fully trade-offs, interactions, and assumptions about the future probably decreased the effectiveness of her recommendations and certainly caused concern among the personnel affected. If for no other reason than information intensity, her problem appears to justify the use of DSS.

How Are DSS Currently Facilitating Tactical Decision Making?

Because of the uniqueness of each Decision Support System, it is not possible to describe a "typical" design, nor is a comprehensive review of DSS applications in institutional settings possible within the scope of this chapter (for reviews, see Bleau, 1981; Hopkins and Massy, 1981). To offer a sense of how DSS are currently facilitating tactical decision making in institutions, this section will describe briefly several general features and capabilities and then illustrate these with a variety of current applications.

Dubey (1984) suggested dividing DSS features into two categories: *data-oriented* and *model-oriented.* Data-oriented systems are intended to augment managerial memory and enhance analytic ability. They allow data to be retrieved, organized, manipulated, analyzed, and displayed according to the needs and preferences of the user. Data retrieval is not a trivial problem when information must be drawn from several databases with differing formats. Likewise, even routine computations may become complicated by alternative analytical approaches (for example, inflated dollars, discounted dollars, staff-years to dollars) and output structures (for example, by fiscal year, by program, by cost category, or by benefit category). Flexible data-oriented systems allow administrators to integrate, manipulate, and organize data with great ease, producing trends and projections in vivid graphic displays.

Model-oriented systems can be looked upon as extensions of an administrator's reasoning and judgment. Several different types are available. *Multiattribute utility models* (illustrated in Chapter Four) are explicit representations of the judgment policies that individual decision makers implicitly use as they make critical choices demanding trade-offs in competing interests. These can be made explicit so that administrators can gain better insight about their own preference. *Simulation models* (illustrated in Chapters Three and Seven) are computer-based representations of specific problem domains that allow individuals to experiment with policies before actually intervening in the real situation. Such models incorporate those organizational characteristics that are judged to be relevant to the impact of policy change. *Interactive optimization models* (illustrated in Chapter Six) differ from the earlier operations research applications only in that conditions of optimality can be easily redefined by individuals as they work with the system. Thus, the consequences of restructuring the model or changing parameters ("sensitivity analyses") can be easily examined. Insofar as part of a semi-structured tactical problem may have one best solution, optimization models may be applicable. Finally, some DSS contain *suggestion model* systems that may alert decision makers to options or considerations that may have been overlooked, that may monitor a large number of changes and flag the more interesting and important ones for special attention, and that may expose administrators to provocative questions that flow from a historical perspective on work similar to that in question.

Dubey (1984) has discussed the application of DSS to the problems faced by library managers who find themselves involved in complicated resource-sharing networks. In order to understand the full cost of network membership versus independence, such managers need to assess the performance of various networks and of their individual libraries. Consequently, they need to know the probabilities, average waiting times, and costs of satisfying various demands. Dubey described a Decision Support System developed at the School of Library and Information Sciences, University of Pittsburgh, using simulation, optimization, and suggestion modeling techniques to aid library managers in their decision-making activities. MODEL simulates the resources (tangible entities such as personnel, terminals, shelf space, and so forth) consumed in performing the various work functions necessary to satisfy each type of demand (transaction). Incorporated into MODEL is a set of policies representing the logical and quantitative decisions that affect the model's flow. MODEL interacts with ECOMODEL, which manipulates cost data, and both interact with a statistical analysis package (SPSS) that feeds into a report generator. Among the managerial questions being posed are the following. Which configuration of network members will result in the fastest service? Which will provide the most economical service? What are the costs and number of personnel necessary to change the mode of processing data? If demands are increased by 50 percent in one area (interlibrary loan, for example), what will be the effects on other areas (local circulation or costs of delivering materials, for example)? If funding is increased 20 percent, what will be the impact on service offered? Dubey suggested that, "with the help of the system, the library administrator can examine several alternatives by asking 'what-if' questions and can make decisions by the comparison of alternatives and the evaluation of outcomes" (p. 253). Further, the system is user-friendly, allowing easy fine-tuning of the model to reflect changes in either managerial judgment or conditions in the decision environment.

Schilling (1984) has described the use of a space management system, INSITE II, by Columbia University. This data-oriented system stores, manipulates, and retrieves with a great deal of flexibility information concerning number of rooms, flow area, organization assignments, room use, groups and activities assigned, rank and number of occupants, and maintenance characteristics. Bijl (1983) has also described a system, BADGER (Building Appraisal and Development with Graphic Evaluative Routines), which provides graphic layouts of current buildings and space utilization patterns. Computer drawings and overlays document existing facilities. The spaces occupied by staff or by activities are measured. Staff, space, and equipment can be tracked with annotated drawings (as opposed to lists). A model-based system allows what-if questions to be asked concerning space allocation, facility improvement, and so forth. BADGER and INSITE II appear to represent a step toward helping managers such as Elaine Simpson with their space allocation decisions.

Hales (1984) has reviewed a number of computer-based systems that are widely used to help facility managers control operations and plan for improvements. There are subsystems for tracking space and equipment inventories, for lease management (dates, options, terms), for maintenance management (scheduling and recording work—preventive, deferred, and housekeeping), for project management (planning, scheduling, and control of moves, rearrangements, renovations, and installations), and for capital budgeting (tracking and controlling appropriations for facilities projects). These capabilities are enhanced by subsystems that provide for space projections (both headcount extrapolation and historical trend projections), clustering and stacking (grouping and assigning related activities using mathematical scoring of questionnaires and charts), block layout (physical plotting of activity placement), and cost justification (using various financial planning techniques). Additionally, computer-aided design (CAD) subsystems are being used for visual development of plans and designs for facility improvements. Dynamic three-dimensional displays can be created interactively and used to visualize changes in existing layouts.

Models such as IFPS (Interactive Financial Planning System) and EFPM (Educational Finance Planning Model) are probably among those decision support tools used most widely by institutional financial planners (Suttle, 1984; Timm, 1983; Hopkins and others, 1982; Masland, 1984). These multipurpose models are being used to conduct "what-if" and "how-to" (goal-seeking) analyses involving such problems as how to balance university revenues and expenditures sensitive to enrollment forecasts and how to determine the trade-offs between amounts of faculty pay raises and the number of faculty that can be employed. Additionally, Suttle (1984) has described the use of SuperCalc by Yale University for making decisions regarding undergraduate financial aid. The model is used to calculate historical trends and then, by projecting them into the future, to estimate total tuition income and financial aid expenditures under a variety of conditions (for example, varying assumptions about tuition growth rate, percentage of students receiving aid, and parental income growth rate).

Several other applications of DSS deserve brief mention here. Casemix systems are being used to help large university-based hospitals become more cost-effective by allowing their managers to react positively to current patient data (Imirie, 1984). A straightforward application of linear programming to setting tuition structures has been successfully used by Trout (1983). Decision consequences feedback systems are helping managers of large, private research and development labs to make better decisions regarding the appropriate mix of research projects (Thierauf, 1982; Stephenson and Stephenson, 1983) and could be used in a similar way by managers of large university-based research organizations. Finally, two additional applications, the use of a Markov model for planning workforce reductions and the use of a multiattribute utility model to facilitate faculty tenure decisions, are described in the chapters that follow.

What Are the Benefits and Problems Associated with DSS?

Although faster decisions or a greater number of decisions in a given time may occur, Keen and Scott Morton (1978) and many others have argued strongly that improving the efficiency of decision making is not the primary purpose of a decision support tool. They stress that DSS are intended to improve decision-making *effectiveness.* They note that iteration and experimentation, although messy, are likely to be an essential part of making good decisions. The most striking evidence of decision-making effectiveness would be provided by the actual success of the decisions made—if environmental and organizational effects could be factored out. However, outcomes are not unequivocally related to the effectiveness of the decision-making process. We await clear empirical evidence, based on objective measures, that DSS are being used successfully.

Cost-benefit analysis has often been applied to the evaluation of computer-based systems, but many of the reasons for initiating, designing, and implementing DSS are intangible and qualitative. Since most cost-benefit evaluations of DSS have chosen to adopt a narrow technical perspective of system performance, their accuracy is difficult to evaluate. There is, however, some evidence that DSS can reduce the "shadow" costs of unavailable or poor information and the difficulty caused by the rigid MIS systems (Uhlig and others, 1979; Tapscott, 1982). There is also some evidence that using DSS can improve accountability and help to "sell" decisions (Kling and Scacchi, 1980). Masland (1984) has noted many successful applications of the EFPM modeling system, if one defines a successful use of DSS as one that has been routinized by decision makers and institutionalized by the organization.

DSS are not without problems. Some are of a technical nature, but these can be and are being overcome relatively easily. The most troubling problems are attributable to the way the systems are implemented; without doubt, these will continue. For more than twenty years, observers have been stressing that the most important reason why so much of the computer technology that an organization acquires is not used at all or never fulfills its potential is because of the poor way in which it is introduced into the organization (Argyris, 1971; Keen and Scott Morton, 1978; Uhlig and others, 1979; Kling and Scacchi, 1980; Tapscott, 1982; Masland, 1983, 1984). That this should be even more true for DSS, which threaten to change managerial and organization decision-making processes, may not be surprising. Since DSS represent a decision-making *service,* the needs of the user should guide its design and implementation. Yet, contrary to the urgings of so many advocates of decision support, technology and technicians too often dominate the process. Many systems are technically splendid but do not really meet the decision needs of a particular user in a particular context. Further, DSS designers are too often unaware of or uninterested in the social and political ramifications of powerful decision aids in institutional settings and their effects on the organization (Keen, 1981; Kling and Scacchi, 1980). Operating strictly from a rational perspective, they are often unprepared to help administrators and their institutions to anticipate and adjust to changes of a sociopolitical nature.

Several writers have suggested methods for meeting the implementation challenges brought on by the widespread changes that are likely to result from powerful technological innovations such as integrated DSS. Tapscott (1982) has advocated user-driven design, by which he means that designers and end-users should be brought together at the earliest stages of the process. Users should be actively involved in the assessment of their own needs and in the design, evaluation, and modification of systems. Thierauf (1982) has noted the effective use of executive steering committees, user review groups, and project teams. Masland (1984) found that the presence in the organization of a person who serves as a key integrator has a positive correlation with success. He suggested that an Information Transfer Specialist should be available to help the organization internalize and institutionalize DSS. Keen (1981) also suggested the importance of a high-status internal change agent, who should move slowly so as not to threaten powerful coalitions that might mobilize to block the change effort.

Jedamus (1984) has described an evolutionary process whereby small stand-alone pilot projects are nurtured and bridges slowly built between them. Because development will then be incremental, adjustment to change is likely to be easier. As benefits become obvious, he predicts that specific DSS applications will proliferate and eventually grow into an integrated system. Jedamus notes, however, that the danger of such an evolutionary, incremental process is anarchy. He has argued (as have Norris and Mims, 1984) that active decision support management is essential in order to integrate DSS into a viable, coordinated, institution-wide system. He further suggested that institutional researchers are well suited and well positioned to play the key role of decision support managers. We could not agree more.

References

Argyris, C. "Management Information Systems: The Challenge to Rationality and Emotionality." *Management Science,* 1971, *17* (6), 275-292.

Bijl, A. "BADGER: Building Appraisal and Development with Graphic Evaluative Routines." *Programmed Learning & Educational Technology,* 1983, *20* (1), 81-82.

Bleau, B. L. "Planning Models in Higher Education: Historical Review and Survey of Currently Available Models." *Higher Education,* 1981, *10,* 153-168.

Donovan, J. J., and Madnick, S. E. "Institutional and Ad Hoc Decision Support Systems and their Effective Use." *Data Base,* 1977, *8,* 79-88.

Drucker, P. F. *The Practice of Management.* New York: Harper & Row, 1954.

Dubey, Y. P. "Decision Support System in the Management of Resource-Sharing Networks." *Information Technology and Libraries,* 1984, *3* (3), 245-254.

Galbraith, J. *Organization Design.* Reading, Mass.: Addison-Wesley, 1977.

Hales, H. L. "Available Computer Technologies." *CEFP Journal,* 1984, *22* (4), 7-11.

Hopkins, D. S. P., and Massy, W. F. *Planning Models for Colleges and Universities.* Palo Alto, Calif.: Stanford University Press, 1981.

Hopkins, D. S. P., Lawrence, L. L., Sonenstein, B., and Tschectelin, J. D. "Financial Modeling: Four Success Stories." *EDUCOM Bulletin,* 1982, *17* (3), 11-16.

Imirie, J. F. "Information System Needs of University-Based Hospitals." *Computers in Healthcare,* 1984, *5* (1), 44.

Jedamus, P. "The Case for Decision Support Management." In W. L. Tetlow (Ed.), *Using Microcomputers for Planning and Management Support.* New Directions for Institutional Research, no. 44. San Francisco: Jossey-Bass, 1984.

Keen, P. "Information Systems and Organizational Change." *Communications of the ACM,* 1981, *24* (1), 24.

Keen, P., and Scott Morton, M. S. *Decision Support Systems: An Organizational Perspective.* Reading, Mass.: Addison-Wesley, 1978.

Kling, R., and Scacchi, W. "Computing as Social Action: The Social Dynamics of Computing in Complex Organizations." In M. Yovitts (Ed.), *Advances in Computers.* New York: Academic Press, 1980.

Masland, A. T. "Simulators, Myth, and Ritual in Higher Education." *Research in Higher Education,* 1983, *18* (2), 161-178.

Masland, A. T. "Integrators and Decision Support System Success in Higher Education." *Research in Higher Education,* 1984, *20* (2), 211-233.

Mason, R., and Mitroff, I. *Challenging Strategic Planning Assumptions.* New York: Wiley, 1981.

Norris, D. M., and Mims, R. S. "A New Maturity for Institutional Planning and Information Management." *Journal of Higher Education,* 1984, *55* (6).

Schilling, G. "Selecting a Space Inventory System: A Case for Flexibility." *CEFP Journal,* 1984, *22* (4), 12.

Simon, H. A. *The New Science of Management Decision.* New York: Harper & Row, 1960.

Stephenson, R. W., and Stephenson, M. K. "Design Requirements for Decision Support Systems for RDT&E." *Information Processing and Management,* 1983, *19* (6), 391-397.

Suttle, J. L. "Using Microcomputers for Institutional Research." In W. L. Tetlow (Ed.), *Using Microcomputers for Planning and Management Support.* New Directions for Institutional Research, no. 44. San Francisco: Jossey-Bass, 1984.

Tapscott, D. *Office Automation.* New York: Plenum, 1982.

Thierauf, R. J. *Decision Support Systems for Effective Planning and Control.* Englewood Cliffs, N.J.: Prentice-Hall, 1982.

Timm, N. H. "Developing a Management Support System in Higher Education." *Planning for Higher Education,* 1983, *11* (2), 27-33.

Trout, M. D. "Deciding Tuition Structure with Linear Programming." *Research in Higher Education,* 1983, *18* (3), 359-371.

Uhlig, R., Farber, O., and Bair, J. *The Office of the Future.* New York: North Holland, 1979.

Joel I. Harmon is assistant professor in the Graduate School of Management at Rutgers, The State University of New Jersey.

A Markov-based decision support application can assist academic administrators in forecasting work-force needs and planning required reductions in force.

Markov Models and Reductions in Work Force

James A. Feldt

In the recent past it was possible for administrators of institutions of higher education to wait for and then react to demands from their resource environments. The environment was at least benign, and more often bountiful. Today the situation has changed: The research environment has become more turbulent, less predictable, and sometimes hostile. These times demand that administrators move from a reactive to an anticipatory mode of management. Fortunately, the technology exists to aid administrators in developing a more active management style. The proliferation of microcomputers has placed within the reach of virtually all administrators the ability to anticipate changes and new demands and to predict the likely effects of a series of alternative policy decisions.

Decisions concerning personnel are among the most common and most difficult choices confronting managers of institutions. This chapter explains how Markov modeling, a straightforward analytical approach, can better inform decision making regarding reductions in work force and other types of personnel decisions.

Reductions in Force

During the years of growth in higher education, the most common personnel problem confronting managers was finding qualified persons

J. Rohrbaugh, A. T. McCartt (Eds.). *Applying Decision Support Systems in Higher Education.* New Directions for Institutional Research, no. 49. San Francisco: Jossey-Bass, March 1986.

to meet rapidly expanding institutional needs while also satisfying internally or externally required affirmative action goals. More recently, the problem facing administrators has been how to reduce the size of the work force. Administrators often bring to this unpleasant task a dearth of experience and a lack of knowledge concerning the types of information needed to make intelligent decisions. They often need assistance in formulating policies that will minimize disruptions to the operations of their institutions, maintain the quality of education, and appear fair and reasonable to the college community.

A number of environmental factors have led to the need for institutions to reconsider the size of their work forces. Demographic patterns in the United States and other developed countries have shifted; the maturation of the "baby boom" generation and reduced birth rates have resulted in substantial reductions in the size of the traditional student population. This smaller pool of students has resulted in increased competition among schools for the most promising students, in an effort to maintain enrollments. The problems caused by the shrinking student population have been exacerbated by changes in federal and state policies regarding funding for higher education. Cutbacks in many areas of government support and inflation in institutional costs have forced most universities and colleges to reexamine their operations. Although some institutions are more affected by these adverse trends than others, all academic administrators must begin to manage personnel more efficiently and prepare for required reductions in the work force in the best way possible. The literature in institutional research has reflected a growing awareness of the need to adjust management strategies to cope with diminishing resources (Alm and others, 1977; Mingle, 1981; Mortimer and Tierney, 1979).

The comparatively recent interest in the management of decline in higher education has been spurred by the experiences of state and local governments beginning in the mid-1970s (Levine, 1978, 1979). During the past decade many political institutions have had to reduce the work force in order to avoid budget deficits. Public administrators have often been poorly prepared to deal with the situation, and cutbacks have frequently been characterized by a heavy-handed approach. Because managers have often had to react at virtually the last moment to demands to cut expenditures, they have been forced to make relatively uninformed decisions concerning layoffs (Greenhalgh and McKersie, 1980). The response has typically been a reactive management approach, which did not allow for planning or systematic analysis. The experiences of public sector administrators point to the need for computerized decision support systems in institutions to aid in the management of decline and necessary reductions in work force.

Markov Models

The term "Markov processes" is named for the Russian mathematician, Andrei Andreevich Markov. Markov's work with the law of large numbers, the central limit theorem, and stochastic processes helped to establish the framework for modern probability theory. Markov developed his work on probabilistic processes from a theoretical perspective, but his work has been widely applied in the study of physical and social phenomena (Olinick, 1978, pp. 304–306).

Markov processes examine the evolution of systems or phenomena where the state of the system at any point in time cannot be determined with certainty. The subjects in the system move among various states according to a set of "transition probabilities." A transition probability represents the likelihood of moving from a state in a given time period to a state in the next time period. The heart of a Markov process model is the matrix of these probabilities. This discussion will deal with one class of Markov models, often referred to as "Markov chains with stationary transition probabilities." In this type of Markov model, three assumptions are made. First, the number of states must be finite, and the states must be mutually exclusive and collectively exhaustive. That is, each subject must fit into only one state or category at a time, and, taken together, the states must account for all of the subjects. Second, it is assumed that the transition probabilities remain constant during the time period of interest. Third, the probability of being in a state at any one time period depends solely on the state of the system in the prior period.

The modeling process can best be understood through a simple example. Assume that all registered voters in a given political unit fall into one of three categories: Democrats, Republicans, and Independents. In order to keep the example simple, also assume that the population of voters is constant for the time period of interest. If one wanted to project the number of voters registered in each category over the next three years, a Markov model would be one appropriate tool to derive these projections. Based on historical data, transition probabilities could be estimated for the likelihood that voters in each party would change to another party in any year. Table 1 provides a hypothetical transition matrix. Note that the probabilities in each row always add up to 1.00, ensuring that all possible movements for a state are included in the analysis. The first row of the table can be interpreted in the following way. It is expected that 80 percent of the Democrats will still be Democrats at the end of any given year. Fifteen percent of the Democrats will change their registration to the Republican party, and 5 percent will become Independents.

Given this matrix and the current number of voters registered in each party, the membership of each party at the end of each year can be

Table 1. Probability Transition Matrix

To:	*Democrats*	*Republicans*	*Independents*
From:			
Democrats	.80	.15	.05
Republicans	.01	.95	.04
Independents	.15	.15	.70

estimated. The mathematical calculations involved will be described in more detail later in this chapter.

Modeling in the Work Force

Markov modeling also provides a means by which one can examine the likely effects of a policy on the future of a work force. In order to use this technique, two sets of data are needed. First, information must be collected on the current status of the system. These data are usually available in a personnel or finance office. Second, a set of probabilities must be generated for the likelihood of the subjects in the system making a transition from one state in a given period to another state in the following period. The Markov approach creates a chain from the current situation into the future, always assuming that the set of probabilities continues to hold true.

Information on the current status of the work force under study must separate the employees into mutually exclusive categories. For example, in studying academic personnel, each faculty member must be assigned to one and only one category. The classification might be: instructors, assistant professors, associate professors, and full professors. If this categorization does not account for all of the faculty members, then additional categories would be needed. In developing a classification scheme, the logical place to start is the campus personnel office's employee categories or codes.

The second set of required data concerns the probabilities that employees would move from one category to another or leave the employment of the college during a time period. These probabilities comprise the set of transition probabilities. Personnel office records are likely to prove useful in deriving these data. Given the time period of interest, such as a fiscal year, probabilities must be established for each category—the proportion of the employees that will remain in that category, the proportion that will leave employment (that is, retire, be dismissed, leave voluntarily, or die) and the proportion that will move into one of the other categories through promotions, transfers, or demotions.

Since the analysis will use the transition probabilities to project the work-force distribution into the future, the set of probabilities should be as accurate as possible. It will probably be helpful to review personnel records for several prior time periods to obtain historical data. The data from several years could be averaged to obtain an estimate for year-to-year fluctuations. If no data are available, it will be necessary to obtain informed estimates from available "experts." Staff in the personnel office, for example, may be able to provide fairly reliable estimates based on their experience.

A Career Ladder Example

Let us assume that the problem concerns only part of the total work force, the maintenance and cleaning staff. The task is to reduce the size of this staff. Assume as well that the files and records of the personnel office contain the job titles and the current number of employees having each of these titles. There are currently 40 senior grade, 100 general grade, and 60 entry grade maintenance workers. Together with a category for persons who leave the university, these three titles constitute the universe of possibilities for the system's state. A maintenance worker will either be in one of the job grades or will no longer be employed by the institution. In this example it is assumed that maintenance workers do not move to jobs performing other functions at the institutions; in more complex models, such movements would have to be taken into account.

The data on the transition probabilities are obtained by reviewing personnel files for, say, the past four years and then asking "experts" to review the probabilities to see if they seem to be reasonable. The matrix of the transition probabilities is shown in Table 2.

According to Table 2, 20 percent of the employees in the entry grade positions in any given year are expected to be in the entry grade a year later. Forty percent of the entry grade employees in that year are expected to be promoted to the general maintenance grade. None of the entry grade employees will go to the senior grade in one year, and 40 percent of the entry grade employees will leave during the year. The "Leave" category

Table 2. Transition Probabilities

To:	*Entry*	*General*	*Senior*	*Leave*
From:				
Entry grade	.20	.40	.00	.40
General grade	.00	.70	.05	.25
Senior grade	.00	.05	.85	.10
Leave	.00	.00	.00	1.00

would include resignations, retirements, deaths, dismissals, and all other forms of leaving employment. Note that these four probabilities (.2, .4, 0, .4) sum to 1.00, indicating that all possible movements for the entry grade employees have been accounted for. Of the general maintenance grade employees, none are demoted to the lower grade during a year, while 70 percent remain in that grade. Five percent of the general grade employees are promoted to senior level, and 25 percent leave employment for some reason during the year. Among the senior grade employees, 5 percent are demoted to general maintenance workers, 85 percent remain on the job in the same grade, and 10 percent leave employment during the year. The last row in the table indicates what happens to persons who have left employment. The "1.00" in the last column indicates that once persons have left employment, they are not rehired. This category is termed an "absorbing state," because an individual who enters the category cannot move to another state. If the model were simulated far enough into the future, every employee would eventually be absorbed into this state.

Given the transition probabilities, it is now possible to track movements in the system from year to year, assuming that the future flow of employees among categories will remain steady. Let us start by exploring a simple across-the-board hiring freeze to determine what effects the policy would have on the work force distribution over time. We can review the results for each year to determine whether the policy has lowered the work force levels by the desired amount and whether unintended consequences have arisen.

The matrix multiplication involved in the calculation of the transitions from year to year and the resulting work force distributions are tedious to perform by hand but straightforward for a computer to calculate. The mechanics of matrix multiplication are not shown here but can be reviewed in any number of texts on quantitative techniques for managers (for example, see Levin and Kirkpatrick, 1978). To assist the reader in following the process, the calculations involved in moving from the base year to year 1 are presented here.

The movements within each of the employee categories are derived by multiplying the number of employees in the category by the row of probabilities appropriate to that category. The forecasted work force distribution is then obtained by summing the appropriate numbers. At the beginning of the base year, the 200 members of the maintenance work force are distributed as follows: 60 entry level, 100 general level, and 40 senior level. Based on the probabilities in the first row of Table 1 and this baseline distribution, the new distribution at the end of the first year is derived. The distribution of 60 entry level workers at the end of the first year is as follows: 12 would still be in the entry level grade (60 times .2); 24 would have been promoted to general maintenance workers (60 times .4); none would be senior workers (60 times .0); and 24 would no longer be employed (60 times

.4). Of the 100 general maintenance workers, 70 would still be in the same grade, 5 would have been promoted to senior level, and 25 would have left through attrition. Of the 40 senior grade employees, 2 would have been demoted to general grade, 34 would still be in the same grade, and 4 would have left employment. By summing the new members of each grade level, one can arrive at the work-force distribution at the end of the first year. There would be 12 entry level workers, 96 general grade workers—24 entry grade employees promoted to the general grade, plus 70 employees who remain general grade employees after one year, plus 2 employees demoted from the senior grade—and 39 senior grade workers (5 + 34 = 39). Fifty-three employees would have left the work force during the year (24 entry level, 25 general level, and 4 senior level).

The transition probabilities are applied to the work-force distribution from the end of the first year to determine movements among the grade levels during the ensuing year, and so on. It should be stressed that this technique assumes that the changes in one year do not alter the transition flows in succeeding years. The resulting work-force distributions for the base year and four future years are shown in Table 3. The numbers shown in the table have been rounded off to the nearest integer value.

Interpreting the Results

This small example demonstrates how the logic of the Markov model is used to arrive at forecasts of the work-force distribution. What lessons can be learned from this particular type of application? A quick review of the work-force distributions in Table 3 produces the following observations. Under the policy of a hiring freeze and the assumptions of static promotion opportunities and terminations, the very high attrition rate and promotion rate for entry level employees quickly reduces that category to zero. The low attrition rate for senior maintenance workers, combined with the continued opportunity for general level workers to advance to the senior grade, results in almost no reduction in the number of senior grade employees. The number of general grade workers falls fairly quickly after the first year, largely because there are no entry level employees being promoted. These

Table 3. Forecasted Work-Force Distributions

	Base Year	*Year 1*	*Year 2*	*Year 3*	*Year 4*
Entry	60	12	2	0	0
General	100	96	74	55	40
Senior	40	39	38	36	34
Total	200	147	114	91	74

dramatic effects of a hiring freeze may not have been evident from the raw data collected but are revealed by the modeling process.

One may now ask whether a policy of reducing the work force through an across-the-board hiring freeze and attrition appears to be successful. The answer, of course, is that the freeze has been successful in reducing the work force; by the end of two years it has been cut almost in half. The results of the model, however, indicate that one may need to ask questions that are more tightly framed. What, in fact, was the goal to be achieved? Was it merely to reduce the total number of maintenance employees? Was the goal to reduce the number of employees, while maintaining roughly the same distribution of workers among entry, general, and senior grades? Or, was the goal to save as much money as possible through reductions in the size of the maintenance staff? One of the most important advantages of a decision support model may be the ability it provides decision makers to cycle back and ask more clearly focused questions, ultimately resulting in more useful analyses.

What other policy might one want to explore, given the results of the first cut at the problem? Administrators may still wish to avoid layoffs. They may also feel, however, that the present model results in an undesirable work-force distribution because the proportion of senior grade workers is too large and the total work force too small by the end of three years. In an effort to address these concerns, the following policy might be tested. First, incentives might be offered to induce senior and general grade workers to retire early. Staff in the personnel office could use records of employee age and length of service to estimate the increased number of employees in the two grades that might be expected to retire each year. As the probability of leaving employment is increased for an employee category, the other probabilities would need to be adjusted to assure that the sum of the probabilities in any row equals 1.00. One might also wish to modify present promotion policies, so as to reduce or eliminate promotion opportunities for general grade workers. This policy revision would then be translated into altered transition probabilities. It would also be possible to examine the effects of hiring a limited number of entry level employees. Setting the number of new hires at a specific level would provide the institution with a means of maintaining a more even distribution of workers across the three grades. The effects of these three changes in policy could be simulated separately or in combination. In the following discussion, the implications of a second policy combining these three strategies will be investigated with a Markov model.

Modeling the Second Policy

Table 4 reflects the transition probabilities incorporating the new retirement and promotion policies. The first row of this table is identical to the table of transition probabilities for the policy of a hiring freeze

Table 4. Transition Probabilities Under the Second Policy

To:	Entry	General	Senior	Leave
From:				
Entry	.20	.40	.00	.40
General	.00	.68	.02	.30
Senior	.00	.05	.80	.15
Leave	.00	.00	.00	1.00

(Table 2). The policy being investigated does not change any of these values for the entry grade employees. The overall new policy will entail hiring 20 new entry level employees each year, but these hires are not reflected in the matrix of transition probabilities.

The row of probabilities for the general grade employees reflects the inducements for early retirement and the limitations on promotions to the senior level. The rate or probability of promotions is to be cut by 60 percent, from .05 to only .02. The probability of general grade employees leaving employment is increased by 20 percent, from .25 to .30. This change reflects an increase in the number of persons retiring and an increase in resignations because of the reduced opportunity for promotion. These two alterations in probabilities mean that the probability of remaining a general grade employee from year to year is reduced from .70 to .68. Note that probabilities in the row still total 1.00. The row of probabilities for the senior employees indicates that the probability of leaving is expected to increase from .10 to .15, due to the early retirement incentives. The probability of remaining in the grade becomes .80.

The calculations for the model would be performed in the manner described previously, with one exception. The work-force distribution for the base year is still multiplied by the set of transition probabilities in Table 4 to determine the makeup of the work force at the end of the first year. The calculations for future years, however, would be adjusted to allow for the new policy of hiring twenty entry level employees each year. Twenty new employees would be added to the entry level grade prior to multiplication by the transition probability matrix to arrive at the work-force levels at the end of successive years. The results for four years are shown in Table 5 below.

Comparison of the Results of the Two Policies

Let us review the work-force distributions resulting from the two policies and examine the funds that would be expended for salaries and fringe benefits under both policies.

Table 5. Forecasted Work-Force Distributions for the Second Policy

	Year 0	*Year 1*	*Year 2*	*Year 3*	*Year 4*
Entry	60	32	26	25	25
General	100	94	79	66	56
Senior	40	34	29	24	20
Total	200	160	134	115	101

The set of pie charts in Figure 1 shows three distributions of the work force. The upper pie chart shows the current (or base year) proportion of maintenance workers in each of the three grades. The two lower charts show the distribution of the work force at the beginning of the fifth year under the first and second policies.

An examination of the three charts reveals that both policies bring about changes in the distribution of the work force. The first policy, a hiring freeze, would create the greatest alteration in the initial pattern of distribution. There would be no entry grade employees, and the senior grade employees would comprise nearly half the work force. Compared with the workers in the two lower grades, employees in the senior grade would receive higher salaries and would probably be more skilled and older on the average. One implication of this policy is that some employees would have to perform jobs more appropriately done by junior workers. The second policy (incentives for early retirement, limited promotion opportunities, and limited new hires at the entry level) would produce more moderate changes in work-force distribution. The proportion of entry level employees would fall from 30 percent to 25 percent of the workers, and the proportion of general grade employees would increase to 55 percent. The percentage of higher-salaried senior level employees would remain at 20 percent of the work force. Clearly, the second policy better maintains the current proportional mix of employees, but the overall size of the work force also shrinks at a slower rate.

In Table 6, hypothetical expenditures for salaries and associated fringe benefits are shown for each policy. The table shows the amount of money expended initially and at the beginning of the fifth year under each policy. The dollar amounts in the table are thousands of constant dollars; that is, the effects of inflation are held constant. The total cost figures are based on the average salary and fringe benefit amount for each grade (obtained from the finance office) and the number of persons in the grades.

Initially, $2,590,000 is spent on the maintenance work force, with 22 percent of the total expenditures going for entry grade employees and 28 percent for senior grade employees. After four years of the first policy, expenditures would fall to $1,132,000, with more than half of the budgeted

Figure 1. Distribution of Employees

INITIAL WORKFORCE DISTRIBUTION

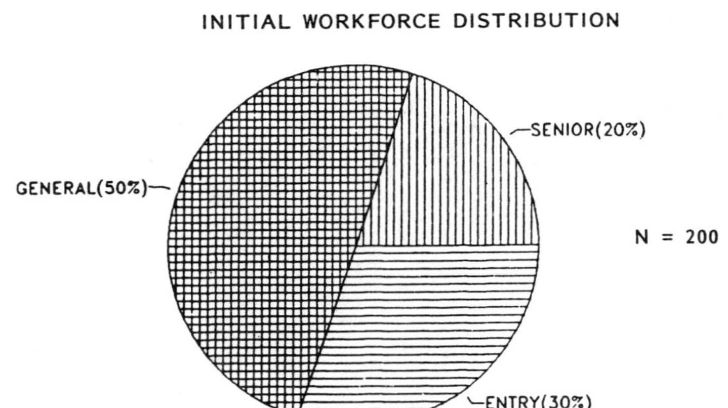

N = 200

DISTRIBUTION AFTER FOUR YEARS
OF THE FIRST POLICY

SENIOR(46%)

N = 74

GENERAL(54%)

DISTRIBUTION AFTER FOUR YEARS
OF THE SECOND POLICY

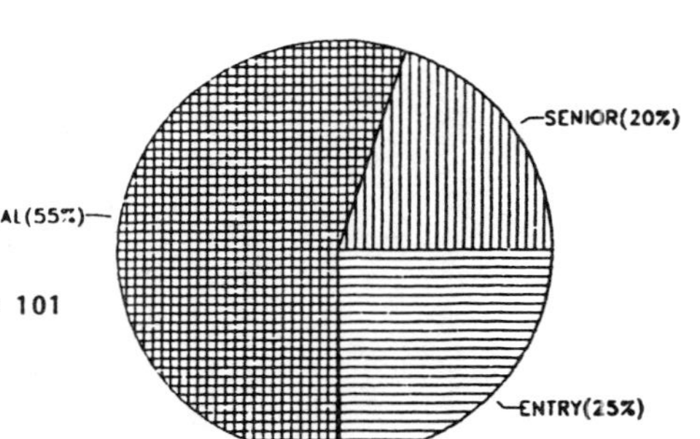

N = 101

Table 6. Salary and Fringe Benefit Expenditures (in thousands of constant dollars)

	Average Cost	*Initially*		*First Policy*		*Second Policy*	
		Number	*Cost*	*Number*	*Cost*	*Number*	*Cost*
Entry	$ 9.5	60	$ 570	0	$ 0	25	$ 237.5
General	13.0	100	1,300	40	520	56	728
Senior	18.0	40	720	34	612	20	360
Total		200	$2,590	74	$1,132	101	$1,325.5

money spent on senior grade employees. Under the second policy, expenditures would be reduced to $1,325,500. The proportion of funds spent on each of the grade levels would be comparable to the initial proportional distribution.

Table 7 reveals another consequence of the two policies. The table shows the average cost per maintenance worker initially and after four years of each policy. This amount is calculated by dividing the total expenditures for maintenance workers by the total number of workers employed (Table 6). The first policy brings about a dramatic increase in the cost per employee, because the work force is comprised of only senior and general grade employees, with senior grade employees making up a very large proportion. The second policy produces a very small percentage increase in the average employee cost.

To summarize the comparison of the two policies, the across-the-board hiring freeze causes a rapid decline in the total number of employees but produces negative consequences that the institution will likely wish to avoid. The work force after four years will be composed entirely of higher-salaried employees and will probably be older on average. More experienced and highly salaried employees will be forced to perform tasks below their level of skill. The much higher cost per employee under Policy 1 expresses in a most succinct manner the overall effect of the policy. Under Policy 2, the size of the total workforce is reduced much more slowly. However, the combination of incentives for early retirement, limits on promotions for general grade employees, and the continued hiring of a small number of entry level employees produce a more even distribution among the three grades. The cost per employee after four years shows almost no increase over the initial average cost. To gain a more balanced perspective, other costs incurred under the second policy, such as the anticipated costs of increased early retirement, should be included in the analysis.

If the second policy is not deemed to be acceptable, administrators could continue to explore alternative policies. The results from the second modeling could be used to help reformulate the question under study and another proposed policy, which could in turn be simulated in a similar fashion.

Table 7. Average Cost Per Employee

	Initially	*First Policy*	*Second Policy*
Amount	$12,950	$15,297	$13,124
Increase over initial		18.1%	1.3%

Sensitivity Testing

As consensus begins to form on the optimal approach, it would be wise to perform sensitivity testing of the model. Sensitivity testing involves varying the parameters of the model (for example, the transition probabilities), singly and in combination, and rerunning the computer model to determine whether the results obtained change significantly. If the results of the model are not markedly altered by an increase or decrease in the value of a variable, then the results of the model are insensitive to that variable. If the results of the model are very sensitive to even small changes in the value of a variable, then additional efforts should be undertaken to verify that the correct value for that variable has been incorporated into the analysis. Sensitivity testing in this context can determine which parameters are most critical to obtain accurate predictions of the outcome of the policy.

Conclusion

The example presented in this chapter was intentionally made simple in order to allow the reader to gain an understanding of the logic embedded in a Markov modeling approach. It should be evident that this analytical technique can be used to examine much more complex situations. For example, the Markov approach has been used to estimate the costs of retaining excess or redundant employees on the payroll while using attrition to reduce the number of employees to the desired level (Feldt and Andersen, 1982; Andersen and others, undated). Bartholomew and Forbes (1979) provide a full bibliography and discussion of statistical approaches to manpower planning, including Markov processes.

Computerized decision support models provide an opportunity for an administrator to investigate the implications of a variety of strategies. Even if the results of the modeling process do not alter the policy proposed initially, decision makers will be more fully aware of the anticipated consequences and will feel more comfortable with instituting the policy. Greenhalgh and McKersie (1980) have shown that any layoff policy has various significant costs for the organization and its employees, including persons laid off and those retained on the payroll, which are frequently overlooked by the organization. The ability to investigate alternative approaches to managing and reducing the work force allows administrators to identify a policy which meets the requirements placed on the institution and is as humane as possible to employees.

More generally, this example illustrates some of the benefits derived from the use of decision support systems. The use of these systems can foster collaboration among colleagues, creative use of data and greater understanding of the problems. DSS allow decision makers to adopt an approach to problem solving which employs an iterative process of defining the problem and proposed solutions. The use of DSS can have short-term benefits by improving specific decisions and long-term payoffs by upgrading the decision-making and management processes.

References

Alm, K. G., Ehrle, E. G., and Webster, B. R. "Managing Faculty Reductions." *Journal of Higher Education,* 1977, *48,* 153–163.

Andersen, D., Feldt, J., Kamya, M., and Newhart, C. *Work Force Planning Case Study.* Albany, N.Y.: Nelson A. Rockefeller College of Public Affairs and Policy, State University of New York at Albany, n.d.

Bartholomew, D. J., and Forbes, A. F. *Statistical Techniques for Manpower Planning.* Chichester, England: Wiley, 1979.

Feldt, J. A., and Andersen, D. F. "Attrition Versus Layoffs: How to Estimate the Costs of Holding Employees on Payroll When Savings Are Needed." *Public Administration Review,* 1982, *42* (3), 278–282.

Greenhalgh, L., and McKersie, R. B. "Cost Effectiveness of Alternative Strategies for Cut-back Management." *Public Administration Review,* 1980, *40* (6), 575–584.

Levin, R. I., and Kirkpatrick, C. A. *Quantitative Approaches to Management,* 4th ed. New York: McGraw-Hill, 1978.

Levine, C. H. (Ed.). "Organizational Decline and Cutback Management." *Public Administration Review,* 1978, *38* (2), 1979–183.

Mingle, J. R. (Ed.). *Challenges of Retrenchment.* San Francisco: Jossey-Bass, 1981.

Mortimer, K. P., and Tierney, M. L. *The Three R's of the Eighties: Reduction, Reallocation, and Retrenchment.* AAHE—ERIC/Higher Education Report No. 4. Washington, D.C.: American Association for Higher Education, 1979.

Olinick, M. *An Introduction to Mathematical Models in the Social and Life Sciences.* Reading, Mass.: Addison-Wesley, 1978.

James A. Feldt is a policy and decision analyst with the Institute of Community and Area Development and an adjunct faculty member of the Department of Political Science at the University of Georgia.

A formal decision model is used to develop a decision support system to assist faculties in making personnel decisions that are systematic, explicit, consistent, and retraceable.

Multiattribute Utility Models and the Tenure Process

Anne Taylor McCartt

One common type of tactical decision involves a choice between two or more courses of action that must be evaluated against multiple criteria (that is, attributes, advantages, or objectives). A class of formal decision models exists to assist in making such choices. These models have been termed multicriteria decision models (Zeleny, 1982) or multiattribute utility models (Huber, 1981). Keeney and Raiffa (1976) have provided an excellent introductory text to such models.

Various techniques have been proposed for specifying the parameters contained in such decision models, in particular the method for generating a common utility scale for measuring all of the criteria (Farquhar, 1984). Some techniques require decision makers to specify these parameters directly. While direct elicitation is the most commonly used method, an accurate set of parameters will be obtained only when decision makers are fully aware of their own complex cognitive processes. Introspective reports about preferences and value trade-offs can lead to inaccurate representations of fundamental decision processes; furthermore, they may not be reliable when tested over time (Balzer and others, 1983). Other techniques have been developed to infer parameters indirectly from decision makers' answers to cleverly phrased questions. One technique following the latter approach is called Social Judgment Analysis (SJA) and derives from a

J. Rohrbaugh, A. T. McCartt (Eds.). *Applying Decision Support Systems in Higher Education.* New Directions for Institutional Research, no. 49. San Francisco: Jossey-Bass, March 1986.

relatively large body of research based on social judgment theory (Hammond and Wascoe, 1980; Hammond and others, 1977).

According to social judgment theory, choices between two or more alternatives are based on an individual's implicit judgment "policy" that can be described by a) the importance attached to each criterion (referred to as the "relative weight"), b) the functional relation between each criterion and a common utility scale (referred to as the "function form"), and c) the particular method used to aggregate these parameters to make the overall judgment (referred to as the "organizing principle"). For example, a judgment policy about graduate admission might be described with equal weights placed on two criteria, GRE verbal (.40) and mathematics (.40) scores, both viewed as twice as important as the undergraduate grade-point average (.20). The functional relation between GRE and admission might be positive linear in form (that is, every unit of increase in score improves equally the chance of admission), but the function form for grades might be nonlinear (that is, the difference between a 2.0 and 2.5 means little with respect to admissibility, but the difference between 3.0 and 3.5 may mean a great deal). Researchers have found that individual differences in these aspects of judgment, as well as inconsistencies in the application of judgment policies, lead to disagreement and interpersonal conflict (Brehmer, 1976; Brehmer and Hammond, 1977).

SJA infers the judgment policies of decision makers by eliciting and statistically analyzing a series of their actual judgments. Such judgments are made explicitly in response to a variety of well-specified alternatives. The parameters of a decision model can then be estimated using the multiple regression equation that best predicts the elicited judgments. The criterion (or dependent) variable is the series of judgments that have been made about multiple alternatives, whereas the predictor (or independent) variables reflect how the alternatives were shown to measure against the multiple criteria. The regression equation thus derived provides the organizing principle, as well as the relative weight and function form for each criterion.

This chapter explains social judgment theory as a way of understanding better the evaluation and review processes in institutions and the use of SJA as the basis for developing a specific decision support system for making decisions about tenure.

Evaluation and Review Processes

Faculty members in academic institutions are regularly called upon to evaluate colleagues for the purpose of granting promotion, continuing appointment, renewal of contract, or salary increments for merit. Although the broad review criteria used are generally consistent across institutions (that is, research, teaching, and university service), the interpretation given to these criteria varies across campuses and even across departments within a single institution. Faculty members may differ greatly in their respective judgment policies, even if written guidelines exist. Because faculty members may apply their judgment policies inconsistently, two individuals with similar views may still differ in their evaluation of a particular candidate. This inconsistency, together with real disagreement over academic values, can result in considerable conflict that may confound judgments on subsequent cases. These problems may recur each time a colleague is evaluated.

While one may argue that such review processes are an inextricable part of academic institutional independence and a flexible tool for applying changing academic standards and goals, one could also question the fairness of processes that often involve vague criteria used in inconsistent ways. A fairer process might evolve more clearly defined assessment tools, including more useful methods for measuring performance with respect to institutional criteria that may well vary in importance. The process also might ensure the consistent application of these criteria. While judgments of the quality of a person's work are always somewhat intuitive and subjective, the way in which these judgments are integrated into an overall evaluation can still be explicit, consistent, and retraceable. More explicit policies and procedures would allow for reviews that not only focus on the specific qualifications of each candidate but also facilitate the understanding of academic expectations.

Researchers have discussed the problems introduced by the subjective and inconsistent nature of typical tenure decisions (Nevison, 1980; Gustad, 1961), and the lack of support for the system expressed by many faculty members (Jolson, 1974). Saaty and Ramanujam (1983) review some of the shortcomings inherent in the tenure process at many institutions and call for a more systematic, "objective" method. These authors propose a mathematical approach, the "Analytic Hierarchy Process," which constructs a hierarchical representation of the tenure process and systematically applies a series of pairwise comparisons to arrive at a weighting scheme.

This chapter examines only one type of review process in one academic setting: evaluations for continuing appointment made by librarians at a large public university. Descriptions of three librarians' personal tenure review policies are derived, using the analytic tool of social judgment analysis. Differences among these policies are discussed, along with a model that can facilitate faculty deliberations and support tenure decisions. Finally, the prototype of a decision support system for faculty personnel decisions based on the straightforward use of an automated spreadsheet is presented.

Hierarchical Model of Tenure Judgment

Librarians have had full faculty status at the university for more than a decade, with four academic ranks: Assistant Librarian, Senior Assistant Librarian, Associate Librarian, and Librarian. Librarians are usually appointed at one of the two lower ranks. The tenure process typically begins during a person's fifth year of service.

The academic faculty of the library has extensively revised its criteria and procedures for tenure review several times. The introduction to the specification of criteria states that "the basic quality which must be evident for promotion in academic rank and/or continuing appointment is the ability to perform at a high professional level in areas which contribute to the mission of the institution." Three broad criteria, "intended to serve as general guidelines," are given:

I. *Effectiveness as a Librarian* (essentially job performance and continuing growth and development)

II. *Contributions to the Advancement of the Profession* (participation in professional/scholarly organizations, research and publication, consultancies, presentations)

III. *University Service* (involvement in library or university committees and "appropriate" community organizations).

No specific weights are attached to the three criteria, but "Effectiveness as a Librarian" is stated to be the most important criterion and must be fulfilled "in an outstanding manner." The candidate must also demonstrate "professional activities of high quality" in fulfilling the remaining criteria and "show evidence that such contributions will continue." In short, the library guidelines are very general and allow a great deal of individual discretion in applying the criteria to evaluate candidates seeking continuing appointment.

Three librarians who represented a variety of backgrounds and diverse work experiences were asked to participate in the decision support project. They included a non-tenured Senior Assistant, a tenured Senior Assistant, and a tenured Associate. Of the four library departments, only the Technical Services Department was not represented. All three persons had participated over the years in a series of tenure and promotion decisions.

Project participants identified five important and discriminating dimensions underlying tenure review. Although these were not all-inclusive, they were viewed as the most salient considerations upon which tenure judgments are based. These five dimensions were: (1) Job performance, (2) Educational credentials, (3) Participation in professional or scholarly organizations, (4) Research and publication record, and (5) University service. An additional dimension, library position, was considered but eliminated because of its "configurality." That is, it was felt that identification of a candidate's position (e.g., cataloger) would affect uniquely the way in which the other information would be used to make a decision. To avoid this complexity, the decision support project focused on tenure reviews within a single department, Reference and Collection Development Services, which is by far the largest department.

Two dimensions, quality of job performance and educational credentials, appeared to be similarly defined and well understood by all three librarians. The other three criteria, however, were seen as more complex factors, and the definitions of these criteria required greater specificity. For example, the meaning of a superior research and publication record was not immediately obvious. Evaluation of a candidate's research and publication record is itself a complex judgment, where types of publications and other related activities are of varying importance, and value trade-offs must be made between the quantity and quality of different kinds of scholarly achievement. Therefore, a hierarchical model of tenure judgment was identified by the librarians (see Figure 1), reflecting two levels of evaluation. Prior to an overall tenure judgment based on all five dimensions, three separate sets of judgments are made concerning candidates' university service, participation in professional or scholarly organizations, and research and publication record. These three judgments serve to clarify the precise meaning of high or low performance on the three dimensions.

As seen in Figure 1, the evaluation of participation in professional organizations is based on the extent of an individual's involvement in organizations at the local, state, and national level, while a university service record comprises two criteria, the level of service within the library and service within the wider university community. The research and publication component of the model consists of six criteria: number of presentations at professional meetings, number of library "in-house" publications, number of book reviews, quality of journal or newsletter edited, number of articles in refereed journals, and number of articles in non-refereed journals.

A series of hypothetical tenure cases were presented to the project participants in the four component segments that required judgment (that is, participation in professional organizations, university service, record of research and publication, and overall judgment about tenure). An example of one of these four judgment tasks is shown in Table 1. In this task, each participant was given a series of thirty-six research and publication profiles and asked to evaluate each case with a rating between 1 (very poor record) and 20 (superior record). Judgments above 10 were used to denote "tenurable" cases. The instructions accompanying the task included a precise description of each criterion's range. Participants were asked to assume that the evidence in each case clearly supported the record presented. Of the four judgment tasks, the research and publication task was the most difficult, since participants were required to consider six discrete pieces of information for each candidate (see Figure 1). As is typically the case, the librarians found the exercise increasingly easy as the criteria became more familiar. The amount of time required to finish the four tasks ranged from 20 to 90 minutes.

Figure 1. Hierarchical Tenure Judgment Task

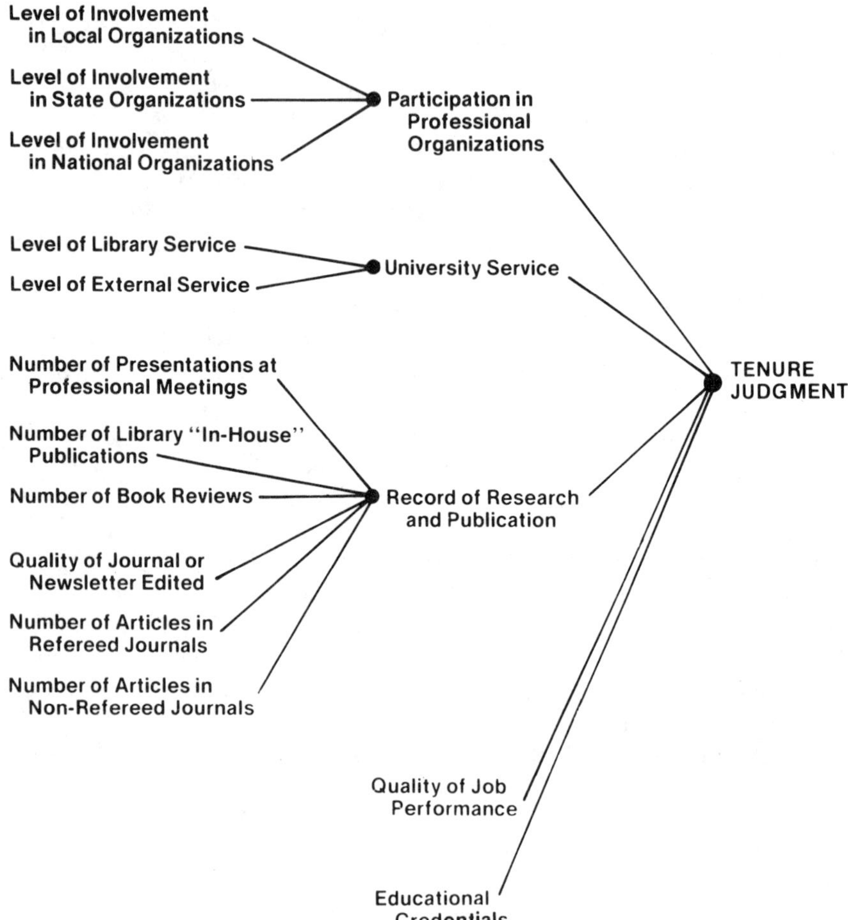

Source: McCartt, 1983. (Reprinted by permission of the American Library Association.)

Table 1. Research and Publication Judgment Task

	Presentations at Professional Meetings	*Library "In-house" Publications*	*Book Reviews*	*Quality of Journal/ Newsletter Edited*	*Articles in Refereed Journals*	*Articles in Non-refereed Journals*
Cases						
1	1	1	14–15	2	1	1
2	2	5	4–6	2	1	4
3	7	1	4–6	1	3	0
4	2	1	2–3	6	0	4
5	2	0	14–15	0	3	3
6	1	5	0–1	5	1	2
7	6	0	12–13	3	1	3
8	0	4	7–9	2	1	2
9	5	2	4–6	3	1	3
10	3	1	7–9	2	1	3
11	2	2	4–6	3	1	0
12	3	1	7–9	3	0	3
13	2	2	7–9	0	2	1
14	3	2	0–1	4	0	3
15	3	0	10–11	1	1	1
16	0	3	2–3	3	0	1
17	4	0	7–9	1	0	3
18	3	0	2–3	4	1	0
19	1	0	10–11	3	0	4
20	4	2	0–1	6	3	1
21	3	0	14–15	5	0	4
22	5	4	14–15	1	0	2
23	5	5	2–3	0	1	3
24	1	0	4–6	4	3	3
25	0	1	10–11	5	2	3
26	2	3	12–13	4	2	2
27	4	4	10–11	4	1	4
28	5	3	10–11	2	3	0
29	4	1	12–13	0	2	4
30	2	4	0–1	3	3	4
31	3	5	10–11	6	3	3
32	6	3	14–15	6	2	3
33	4	5	14–15	3	2	0
34	7	2	10–11	0	0	1
35	3	3	0–1	0	0	2
36	4	0	0–1	1	1	4
Range	0–7	0–5	0–15	0–6	0.3	0–4
Mean	3.1	2.1	7.7	2.7	1.3	2.3

Source: McCartt, 1983. (Reprinted by permission of the American Library Association.)

Descriptions of Various Tenure Review Policies

Descriptions of the four component judgment policies for each participant were derived, using SJA to produce multiple regression equations that allowed for nonlinear function forms where appropriate. For every task, the regression analyses were used to identify the relative weight and function form relating each tenure criterion to the ratings assigned by the librarians. Each regression analysis also produced a multiple correlation coefficient R, an index of the closeness of match between predictions of an individual's judgment that could be made analytically with the use of the regression equation and the person's actual judgments in the same instances. A high multiple R indicates that the model provides a good explicit representation of the implicit judgment policy, that the model can be used to predict future judgments accurately, and that the individual is applying the judgment policy consistently. A low R could be due either to inconsistency on the part of the judge or to the model's failure to represent accurately the full cognitive complexity of an individual's judgment process. The multiple correlation coefficients derived for the four judgment tasks (shown in Table 2) were generally quite high, with only three less than .90 and only one less than .85. This indicates that the judgment models are generally excellent representations of the implicit judgment policies exercised by the three librarians.

One way in which individuals may vary is the number of candidate profiles identified as "tenurable"; some reviewers set a higher standard for tenure than others. As one measure of this standard, the arithmetic means of the judgments made by each librarian on the 20-point rating scale were computed. They are shown in Table 3 for each of the four judgment tasks. In this instance, the differences among judges were relatively small. Interestingly, the mean judgment for tenure for all three judges fell close to 10, the arbitrary cutoff point set for a positive tenure decision.

Individuals may also differ in the relative importance given to a particular criterion. The relative weights for the four judgment tasks are presented in Table 4. Each weight represents the relative contribution of a criterion to the overall judgment. All three judges had similar weighting

Table 2. Multiple Correlation Coefficients

	Judge 1	*Judge 2*	*Judge 3*
Task 1: Organizational Participation	.87	.90	.93
Task 2: University Service	.93	.95	.97
Task 3: Research/Publication	.69	.87	.94
Task 4: Overall Tenure Judgment	.95	.96	.96

Table 3. Mean Judgments

	Judge 1	*Judge 2*	*Judge 3*
Task 1: Organizational Participation	12.7	10.7	11.7
Task 2: University Service	10.4	9.8	10.0
Task 3: Research/Publication	13.5	12.5	12.8
Task 4: Overall Tenure Judgment	9.6	9.6	10.9

Table 4. Relative Weights

	Judge 1	*Judge 2*	*Judge 3*
Task 1: Organizational Participation			
Local Organizations	.28	.32	0
State Organizations	.36	.26	.37
National Organizations	.36	.42	.63
Task 2: University Service			
Library Service	.44	.36	.31
External Service	.56	.64	.69
Task 3: Research/Publication			
Number of Presentations	0	.70	0
Number of "In-House" Publications	.28	0	0
Number of Book Reviews	.24	0	.08
Quality of Journal Edited	.48	0	.23
Number of Refereed Articles	0	.30	.45
Number of Non-Refereed Articles	0	0	.24
Task 4: Overall Tenure Judgment			
Organizational Participation	0	.08	.08
Research/Publication	0	.09	.53
University Service	0	.10	.06
Quality of Job Performance	1.0	.60	.34
Educational Credentials	0	.12	0

schemes for university service. Service external to the library was always weighted more heavily than internal library service, although the weights assigned to external service range from .56 (Judge 1) to .69 (Judge 3). For the organization participation task, Judges 1 and 2 appeared to distribute their weights fairly evenly across the three criteria—level of involvement in local, state, or national organizations. Judge 3, however, assigned no importance to the level of local organizational participation and gave a weight of .63 to activities in national organizations. Not unexpectedly, the judges differed dramatically in their weighting schemes for the research and publication task. None of the judges used all six criteria in rating the research and publication profiles, and Judge 1 and Judge 2 based their judgments on completely different criteria. Judge 2 used only two criteria, the number of presentations at professional meetings and the number of articles in refereed journals. Only Judge 3, using four criteria, indicated the number of articles in refereed journals to be most important.

The three judges also used markedly different weighting schemes in evaluating candidates' overall qualifications for tenure. Judge 1 looked at job performance as the sole criterion when evaluating profiles for tenure. Judge 2 used all five criteria but also placed the greatest importance on job performance (.60). The remaining four criteria all received similar weights, ranging from .09 to .12. Judge 3 used all criteria except educational credentials. Most heavily weighted was the research/publication criterion (.53). Job performance was given a weight of .34, with university service and organizational participation considered much less important at weights of .06 and .08, respectively.

A weighting scheme alone does not completely describe an individual's judgment policy. A second component is the form of the functional relationship between the measure of each criterion and the overall judgment. For the tasks of organizational participation, university service, and tenure, the function forms for the three judges were all increasing, although not all were linear. The function forms for the research and publication record task are presented in Figure 2, along with the relative weights. With the exception of the library publications criterion, the function forms are increasing throughout. That is, the higher the level on the cue, the higher the rating given. The function for number of library publications, used only by Judge 1, decreases up to three publications and then increases. Where relative weights are negligible, no function form can be estimated.

Taken together, the function forms and relative weights in Figure 2 describe three alternative judgment policies about the use of research and publication records in tenure review. As the functions and weights show, the three reviewers have fundamental disagreements over how a particular record of research and publication should be evaluated. For example, a candidate whose activities have been publishing in refereed journals and making presentations at professional meetings would receive a high overall rating from Judge 2, a 0 rating from Judge 1, and a mediocre rating from Judge 3.

Development of a Promotion/Tenure Decision Support System

The results of SJA can serve as the basis for developing a departmental decision support system (DSS) for evaluating candidates for tenure and/or promotion. The system would have two components: an information system on faculty members and a spreadsheet that would convert the performance of a candidate into an overall tenure or promotion score. The system could be created and maintained on a microcomputer. Using

Figure 2. Judgment Policies for Research and Publication Sub-Task

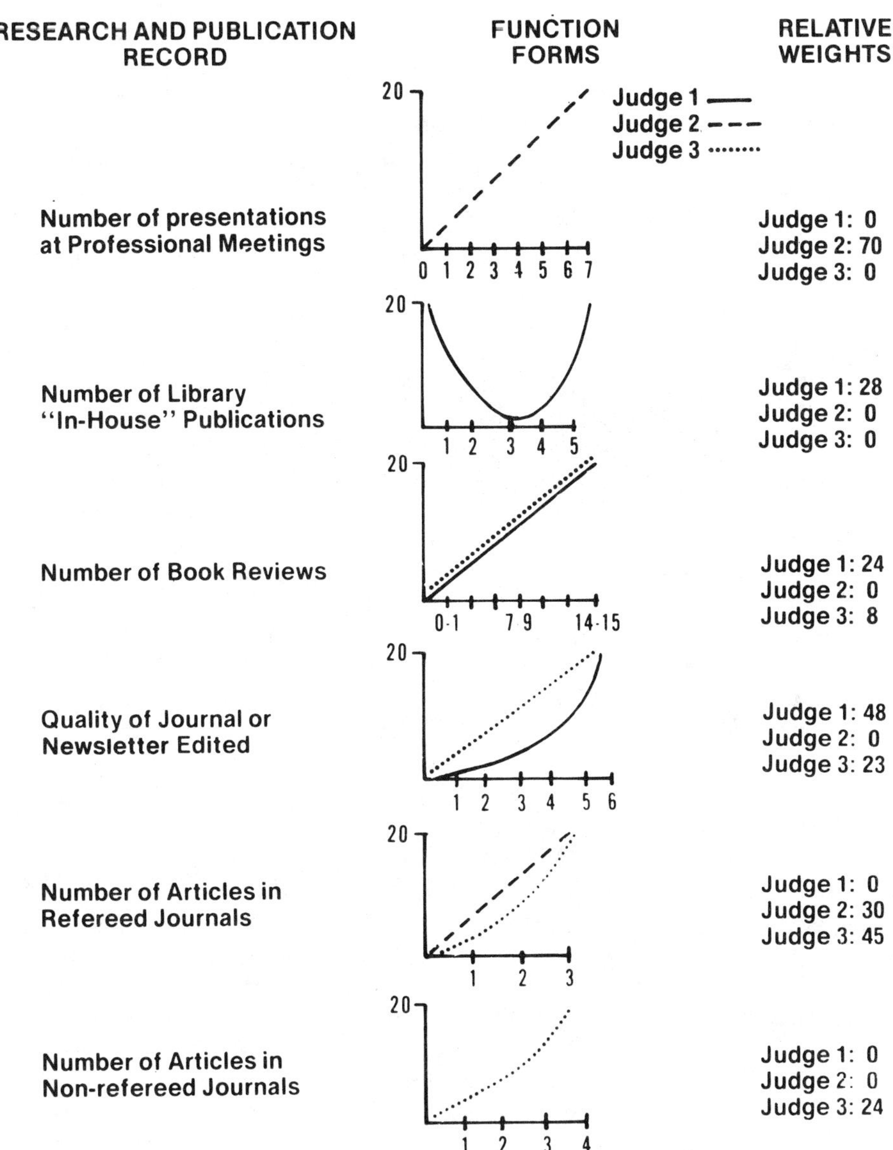

Source: McCartt, 1983. (Reprinted by permission of the American Library Association.)

the criteria embedded in a departmental SJA model, the computerized information system would store relevant descriptive data for faculty members. Although the SJA project reported in this chapter used hypothetical cases, files of historical and current actual case characteristics could be maintained.

The system could serve several purposes. First, when considering a particular candidate for tenure and promotion, the system would provide a structure for collating information on the performance of the candidate; candidates and the department would know what information to gather in preparation for personnel decisions. Second, the system could produce a detailed summary of the accomplishments of departmental faculty at any point in time, and the patterns in accomplishments could be tracked over time. Third, if the system were standardized across departments, campus summary statistics or interdepartmental comparisons could be generated. Thus, the system could assist departmental faculties, campus review committees, administrators, and institutional researchers. It should be noted that the system could contain data on variables that would be useful for administrators or researchers but not for tenure decisions.

For example, taking the research and publication judgment task described above, Figure 3 shows the mean score of Department A's faculty members in 1980 and 1985 for three of the criteria in the model: presentations at professional meetings, articles in refereed journals, and articles in non-refereed journals. For the purpose of this illustration, the cue ranges were increased. The mean number of presentations rose from 4 in 1980 to 7 in 1985, and the mean number of articles published in refereed journals increased from 5 to 6. The mean number of articles appearing in non-refereed journals fell from 5 to 4.

As a further illustration of the system's versatility, Figure 4 presents a comparison of three departments for the same three criteria. The graph shows the mean scores of faculty members granted tenure from 1980 to 1985. The profile for Department A is 6 presentations, 7 publications in refereed journals, and 2 publications in non-refereed journals. Department B faculty had fewer presentations (3) and publications in refereed journals (5) but produced an average of 4 publications in non-refereed journals. Department C had the highest number of articles in non-refered journals (6) and the fewest number of articles in refereed journals (3). Faculty members in Department C made an average of 4 presentations.

The second component of the decision support system is a series of spreadsheets converting the performance of a candidate on the SJA criteria to an overall tenure rating. It is not suggested that this system replace faculty deliberations, but rather that the system serve as the point of departure for faculty discussion of a candidate. The system would reflect departmental faculty consensus on the appropriate weights and function forms for tenure criteria. It would be understood, of course, that the criteria

Figure 3. Department A's Research and Publication Records 1980 versus 1985

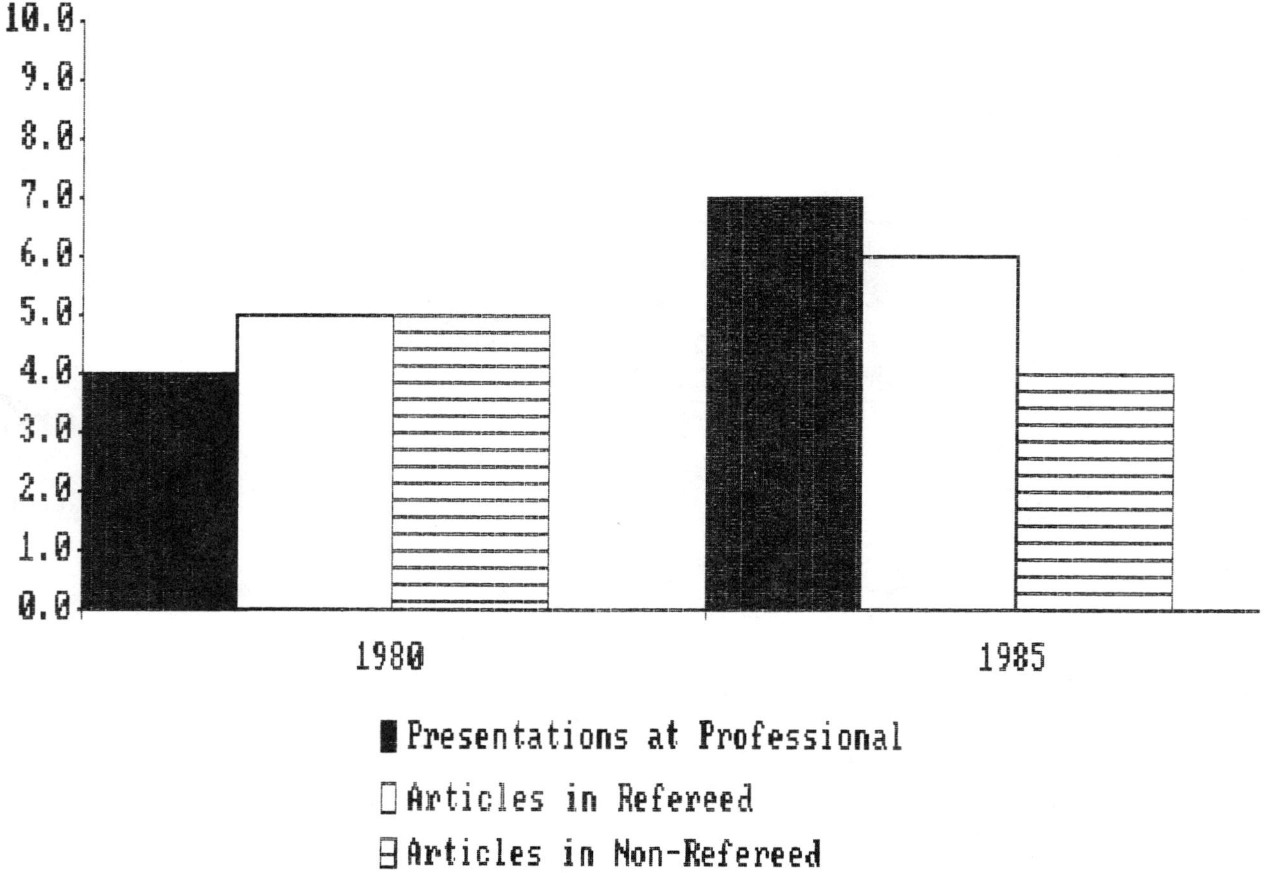

Figure 4. Research and Publication Records of Faculty Granted Tenure Departments A, B, C (1980–1985)

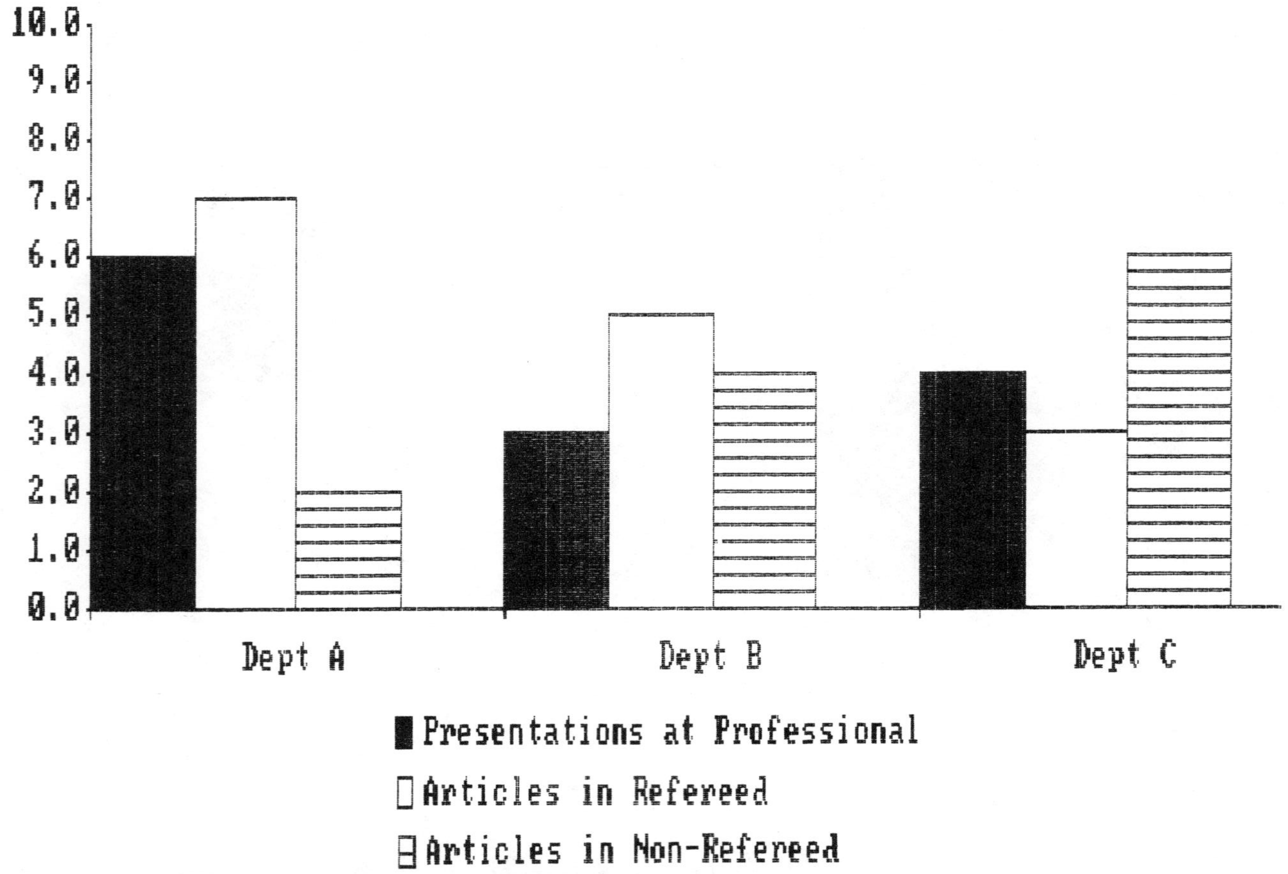

10.0
9.0
8.0
7.0
6.0
5.0
4.0
3.0
2.0
1.0
0.0

Dept A
Dept B
Dept C

Presentations at Professional
Articles in Refereed
Articles in Non-Refereed

could not be inclusive of all possible relevant activities. The consideration of each candidate would focus first on how well the candidate performed against the group judgment model and would then turn to additional relevant aspects of the candidate's record.

Based on the departmental SJA model, a microcomputer spreadsheet can easily be constructed to convert the performance of a particular tenure candidate into a score. Figure 5 shows two spreadsheets developed from the record of a hypothetical candidate and Judge 3's judgment policies. The candidate's performance score for each criterion is shown by an asterisk. The top spreadsheet indicates that this candidate's research and publication record includes 6 presentations at professional meetings, 1 "in-house" publication, 4 to 6 book reviews, editing a newsletter for a local organization, and 3 journal articles (2 in a refereed journal). These data would be retrieved from the information system described above.

Using the weights and function forms derived for Judge 3 in Figure 2, the computer converts each performance score into a rating. To assist the user in interpreting the spreadsheet, the corresponding weighted judgment rating is shown directly under each performance score. The overall rating for research and publication for this candidate is 2.10 (of a possible 6 points). This rating was generated by the computer from the sum of the weighted ratings of 0 for presentations and library publications, .15 for book reviews, .3 for editorship, 1.5 for refereed journal articles, and .15 for non-refereed journal articles.

The second spreadsheet in Figure 6 shows the overall tenure judgment for this hypothetical candidate, again based on Judge 3's judgment policy. The score of 2.10 for research and publication converts into a rating of 3.5 in the overall judgment model, and the candidate receives an overall tenure rating of 9.2 out of 20 possible points. The candidate's case is weakened by a below-average research and publication record. The fact that the candidate has a doctoral degree does not contribute to the overall rating, since a zero weight is given to educational credentials. Unless the faculty had established an absolute cutoff point for tenure, the score of 9.2 does not in itself indicate a decision. Discussion might turn to such accomplishments as consulting, not captured in the model.

The tenure decision support system has unlimited versatility. Any aspect of the model—criteria, weights, or function forms—can be tailored to any department and revised at any point. In Figure 6, for example, a second hypothetical model for the overall tenure judgment places a much greater emphasis on educational credentials and university service. Evaluated against this model, the same candidate achieves a rating of 12.5.

In addition to aiding departmental tenure or promotion deliberations, such a decision support system has other uses. It can provide valuable information to individual faculty members prior to a decision regarding their promotion or tenure. Since departmental expectations

Figure 5. Spreadsheet Based on Judge 3's Judgment Policies

TASK III:RESEARCH AND PUBLICATION RECORD									
1. Number of Presentations at Professional Meetings									
Score	0	1	2	3	4	5	6 *	7	
Rating		Weight=0							0.00
2. Number of Library "In-House" Publications									
Score	0	1 *	2	3	4	5			
Rating		Weight=0							0.00
3. Number of Book Reviews									
Score	0-1	2-3	4-6 *	7-9	10-11	12-13	14-15		
Rating	0	.1	.15	.2	.3	.4	.5		0.15
4. Quality of Newsletter or Journal Edited									
Score	0	1 *	2	3	4	5	6		
Rating	0	.3	.5	.7	.9	1.2	1.4		0.30
5. Number of Article in Refereed Journals									
Score	0	1	2 *	3					
Rating	0	.7	1.5	2.7					1.50
6. Number of Articles in Non-Refereed Journals									
Score	0	1 *	2	3	4				
Rating	0	.15	.4	1	1.4				0.15
					SUB-TASK III RATING				2.10

TASK IV:OVERALL TENURE JUDGMENT								
1. Participation in Professional Organizations								
	Minimal			Moderate		Exceptional		
Score	0	1	2	3 *	4	5	6	
Rating	0	.3	.6	.8	1.1	1.4	1.7	0.80
2. University Service								
	Minimal			Moderate		Exceptional		
Score	0	1	2	3	4	5 *	6	
Rating	0	.2	.3	.6	.8	.9	1.1	0.90
3. Research and Publication Record								
	Poor			Average			Superior	
Score	0	1	2 *	3	4	5	6	
Rating	0	1.7	3.5	5.3	7.0	8.8	10.5	3.50
4. Job Performance								
	Poor			Average			Superior	
Score	0	1	2	3	4 *	5	6	
Rating	0	.7	1.7	2.7	4.0	5.0	6.7	4.00
5. Educational Credentials								
	MLS			MLS & Subject Master's			Doctorate	
Score	0	1	2	3	4	5	6 *	
Rating				Weight=0				0.00
					OVERALL TENURE RATING			9.20

Figure 6. Spreadsheet Based on Revised Judgment Policy

TASK IV:OVERALL TENURE JUDGMENT

1. Participation in Professional Organizations								
	Minimal			Moderate		Exceptional		
Score	0	1	2	3 *	4	5	6	
Rating	0	.4	.7	1	1.4	1.7	2	1.00
2. University Service								
	Minimal			Moderate		Exceptional		
Score	0	1	2	3	4	5 *	6	
Rating	0	.5	1	1.5	2	2.5	3	2.50
3. Research and Publication Record								
	Poor			Average		Superior		
Score	0	1	2 *	3	4	5	6	
Rating	0	1	2	3	4	5	6	2.00
4. Job Performance								
	Poor			Average		Superior		
Score	0	1	2	3	4 *	5	6	
Rating	0	1	2	3	4	5	6	4.00
5. Educational Credentials								
	MLS			MLS & Subject Master's		Doctorate		
Score	0	1	2	3	4	5	6 *	
Rating	0	.5	1	1.5	2	2.5	3	3.00
				OVERALL TENURE RATING				12.50

would be clearly specified, faculty members could more accurately gauge their progress toward meeting those expectations. The system would also provide documentation for a department to support its decisions to a campus-wide faculty review committee or to campus administrators. Finally, a system could be developed for use by higher, campus-wide levels of review.

Conclusion

In this chapter a model was presented that can aid faculty members in making consistent, fair, and systematic personnel decisions. A decision support system was described that would provide current data on faculty members' accomplishments and assist in deliberations on personnel decisions.

Institutional researchers can be instrumental in assuring that such an approach is implemented. First, an office of institutional research could establish a campus-wide, standardized information system to support personnel decisions. Second, the office could develop the spreadsheets for use by a particular department, based on input by the department on the paramenters of the model. Third, the office could advocate the use of such a system and seek to get this innovation adopted by departments and linked to higher levels of decision making.

In addition to decisions concerning tenure or promotion, there are many other areas where institutional researchers could apply SJA techniques. The model presented in this chapter could easily be extended to develop a model for assisting in faculty or administrative appointments. Another application would be a model for evaluating persons applying for admission to the institution. As with the tenure/promotion model, SJA-based DSS would not only assist in making decisions on hiring or admission but could also generate useful summary statistics for adminstrators and institutional researchers. In fact, SJA and other multiattribute utility models will prove useful in structuring any decision involving trade-offs among multiple considerations.

As suggested in Rohrbaugh's introduction to this volume, designers of SJA-based DSS may prefer to start with a problem which is relatively circumscribed and which involves a limited number of decision makers. Once a simple model is in place, it can be adapted to serve additional needs as they arise.

References

Balzer, W. K., Rohrbaugh, J., and Murphy, K. R. "Reliability of Actual and Predicted Judgments Across Time." *Organizational Behavior and Human Performance,* 1983, *32,* 109–123.

Brehmer, B. "Social Judgment Theory and the Analysis of Interpersonal Conflict." *Psychological Bulletin,* 1976, *83,* 985–1001.

Brehmer, B., and Hammond, K. R. "Cognitive Factors in Interpersonal Conflict." In *Negotiations: Social-Psychological Perspectives.* Beverly Hills, Calif.: Sage Publications, 1977.

Farquhar, P. "Utility Assessment Methods." *Management Science,* 1984, *30,* 1283–1300.

Gustad, J. W. "Policies and Practices in Faculty Evaluation." *Educational Record,* 1961, *42,* 194–211.

Hammond, K. R., Rohrbaugh, J., Mumpower, J., and Adelman, L. "Social Judgment Theory: Applications in Policy Formation." In M. F. Kaplan and S. Schwartz (Eds.), *Human Judgment and Decision Processes: Applications in Applied Settings.* New York: Academic Press, 1977.

Hammond, K. R., and Wascoe, E. (Eds.). *Realizations of Brunswik's Representative Design.* New Directions for Methodology of Social and Behavioral Science, no. 3. San Francisco: Jossey-Bass, 1980.

Huber, G. *Managerial Decision Making.* Springfield, Ill.: Scott, Foresman, 1981.

Jolson, M. A. "Criteria for Promotion and Tenure: A Faculty View." *Academy of Management Journal,* 1974, *17,* 149–154.

Keeney, R. L., and Raiffa, H. *Decisions with Multiple Objectives: Preferences and Value Tradeoffs.* New York: Wiley, 1976.

McCartt, A. T. "The Application of Social Judgment Analysis to Library Faculty Tenure Decisions." *College and Research Libraries,* September 1983.

Nevison, C. H. "Effects of Tenure and Retirement Policies on the College Faculty." *Journal of Higher Education,* 1980, *51* (2), 150–166.

Saaty, T. L., and Ramanujam, V. "An Objective Approach to Faculty Promotion and Tenure by the Analytic Hierarchy Process." *Research in Higher Education,* 1983, *18* (3), 311–331.

Zeleny, M. *Multiple Criteria Decision Making.* New York: McGraw-Hill, 1982.

Anne Taylor McCartt is program manager with the Institute for Traffic Safety Management and Research, Rockefeller College of Public Affairs and Policy, State University of New York at Albany.

Part 3.

Strategic Decision Support

Decision conferencing extends the usefulness of DSS to the most difficult problems faced by executive teams.

Strategic Decision Making and Group Decision Support Systems

Michael Robert McGrath

The last major change in group decision making occurred more than 100 years ago when *Robert's Rules* first imposed order on a meeting. The system has placed much otherwise unruly discussion and debate under greater control, but rarely do administrators, even those frustrated by seemingly endless meetings on a consequential policy issue, look to *Robert's Rules* to improve the effectiveness of the decision process. It is recognized that, while mandated procedures may formally structure the communication pattern in a group, they offer little to enhance the content of what is spoken. When the problems faced by a group are unique and particularly complex, its members need more support in their decision making than rules of order.

In the previous section, Harmon, Feldt, and McCartt examined the use of Markov and multiattribute utility models as illustrations of decision support systems for tactical decision making. This section of the sourcebook will turn to strategic decision making and group decision support systems (GDSS) using resource allocation and system dynamics models as illustrations. Given the proliferation of terms in this area, the intent of this overview is to differentiate between tactical and strategic decision mak-

J. Rohrbaugh, A. T. McCartt (Eds.). *Applying Decision Support Systems in Higher Education.* New Directions for Institutional Research, no. 49. San Francisco: Jossey-Bass, March 1986.

ing, examine various innovative types of group decision support systems, and demonstrate the importance of "group" considerations, given the nature of strategic decision making.

Tactical Decision Making and Strategic Decision Making

Clarifying the distinction between tactical and strategic decision making is not an easy task. Like many fields of organizational research, the area of decision making is in dire need of a usable typology. Mintzberg (1982), one of the principal advocates of typology development, viewed the lack of a typology in organizational decision making as one of the greatest blocks to progress in all of organization theory. While there is still no generally accepted typology, several have been suggested in the literature (see Harrison, 1981).

At the minimum, Drucker (1954) stressed the value of distinguishing the concepts of tactical and strategic decision making. Unlike more routine, tactical decisions, Drucker presented strategic decisions as those that "really matter," that "aim at changing the whole situation." In strategic decision making, "the important and difficult job is never to find the right answer; it is to find the right question" (Drucker, 1954, p. 351). The "nonprogrammed" decisions about which Simon (1960) wrote are essentially strategic in quality: novel, unstructured, and consequential. In Simon's words, "There is no cut-and-dried method for handling the problem because it hasn't arisen before, or because its precise nature and structure are elusive or complex, or because it is so important that it deserves a custom-tailored treatment" (1960, p. 5).

Although optimal solutions may be found for tactical problems, the purely rational view of decision making that dominated neoclassical economic theory and influenced the development of operations research and management science does not appear to guide much strategic decision making. Here, there are too many alternatives for acquiring comprehensive information; it is difficult to conduct extensive analyses of their relative merits. Simon (1957) argued convincingly that there are clear limits to human cognition ("bounds" on rationality) that make futile any effort to achieve complete accountability in strategic decision making through "exhaustive" empiricism (for example, building "total systems" to store all relevant data).

"Bounded" rationality admits "satisficing" decision behavior—the identification of an acceptable (not necessarily optimal) alternative course of action. The compromise between the complexity of the problem and the resources available to a decision maker results in a heuristic model of choice, preferably one that is quite efficient to put into use. Such a model is well suited for tactical decisions involving explicit goals. For example, the acquisition of library books for an institution does not need to be an optimal process in order to be effective. Both "exhaustive" empiricism and "bounded" rationality provide a necessary theoretical foundation for much of the development of DSS involving tactical problems (Keen and Scott Morton, 1978, pp. 62–69), but these perspectives are not sufficient for supporting strategic decision making.

Where tactical decision processes can be more readily regulated and explicated through models developed for individual decision makers, strategic decision processes require greater flexibility to deal with the variety of implicit goals, values, and interests of affected parties in the organization. Strategic decision making, in contrast to tactical decision making, is much more political and consensual. Advocacy of and commitment to strategic decisions are essential for successful implementation. Therefore, they depend upon adaptable and participatory group processes that provide ample opportunity for persuasion and accommodation.

Keen and Scott Morton (1978) have emphasized the importance of political and consensual issues to decision support, but they have also noted the extraordinary lack of attention these issues have received in systems development. According to Keen and Scott Morton (1978, p. 71), "most analysts and designers are surprised that it should be seen as relevant." Nevertheless, an early finding in studies of DSS implementation was that they were often used not as tools for individual decision makers but as support for collective, organizational processes (Keen, 1980). In fact, a recent study of DSS in eighteen organizations (Hogue and Watson, 1985) reported that two-thirds of the applications involved two or more individuals jointly making decisions. Because it is common for groups of decision makers faced with strategic problems to rely upon DSS, new methods have been developed to respond to their special and collective needs: group decision support systems (GDSS).

Group Decision Support Systems

Many of the support systems that exist to aid groups in strategic decision making are variants of computer-supported conference rooms (DeSanctis and Gallupe, 1985; Huber, 1984). Kraemer and King (1983) have suggested, however, that there is little agreement among individuals working in this field as to what constitutes a computer-supported conference room. Some common components appear to include personal computer terminals for each participant in the meeting, a public display screen for viewing by the whole group, computing and communications capability between all participants, and computer software for word processing, database access and management, and graphics display. The objectives of computer-supported conference rooms are to make group decision making more effective by increasing both the effectiveness of such meetings and participant satisfaction with the process.

Although solid research is lacking, computer-supported conference rooms appear to reduce process losses in group decision making. These process losses include domination of discussion by particular individuals, deference to high-status participants by lower-status participants, group pressures leading to conformity of thought, miscommunication among members, and inadequate devotion of time to full problem exploration and the generation of possible alternatives, objectives, and scenarios of impending events. In reviewing the wide range of activities that fall under the rubric of computer-supported conference rooms, Kraemer and King (1983) have classified the various forms into four categories: electronic boardrooms, teleconferencing facilities, information centers, and decision conference rooms.

Electronic Boardrooms. These are the most elementary of the designs for computer-supported conference rooms. They differ from their nonelectronic parent only to the extent that audiovisual technology is computer-based (for example, computer graphics, computer-controlled audiovisuals, and immediate word processing.).

Teleconferencing Facilities. These are computer-supported conference rooms designed primarily to facilitate meetings between individuals in different locations. Such facilities are often equipped as electronic boardrooms with the capacity to share information and ideas across sites through the use of advanced audiovisual technology.

Information Centers. These are specially developed facilities that are connected to an organization's data processing center. They are designed especially to support users of computer-based information systems engaged in such activities as generating reports and modifying databases.

Decision Conference Rooms. These settings are constructed specifically for the purpose of bringing decision support systems into meetings of multiple users. They allow for the integration of an organization's information and decision technologies.

Decision conferences differ from the other three forms of computer-supported conference rooms in that they address not only the technological needs of strategic decision making but also the behavioral dynamics that are an integral part of that process. Of all the forms of computer-supported conference rooms currently in use, decision conference rooms hold the most immediate promise of providing administrators with a workable group support system for strategic decision making.

Decision Conferencing

Computer-supported decision conference rooms typically are staffed by professionals whose experience blends two types of decision-making expertise: the information management and operations research skills useful in building decision models and the group dynamics and organizational development skills useful in group facilitation and conflict management

(Quinn and others, 1985; Phillips, 1984; Huber, 1982a). Such staffing aims to integrate rational, empirical, political, and consensual perspectives on effective group decision making. Decision conferences are intensive working sessions that vary in length from a one-day conference to a series of two or three-day conferences; a common format is one two-day decision conference. They are often held in a large meeting room located at a distance from the usual office location of participants, so as to ensure continuity of discussions with minimal interruptions. Meeting rooms are equipped with a microcomputer that can operate either in a stand-alone capacity or as a remote terminal with access to various time-sharing facilities. (Many decision conferences do not require each participant to have a personal CRT and input device.) Meeting rooms also contain several very large white boards, a large-screen video projector for graphic displays from the microcomputer, a letter-quality printer, and a large circular or U-shaped table that can comfortably seat ten to fifteen people.

It is essential that a decision conference include every decision maker who has a significant stake in the outcome of the process, and all participants must be available for the full duration of the meeting. Most conferences involve at least three staff analysts in the process. One analyst, designated as the group facilitator, uses a variety of techniques from group dynamics to assist participants in defining and structuring the focal problem. This portion of the process consists of identifying all relevant issues (such as alternative options and evaluation criteria) and placing these insights on the white boards. At the same time, another analyst enters the same information into the microcomputer using a software package appropriate for the unique structure of the particular problem. As a result, the capacity exists to update and modify immediately the information input as the discussion proceeds. A third analyst concentrates on recording the full rationale that organizational members are offering for their expressed preferences. At the end of the conference, all of this information, along with relevant computer printout, is produced as a single document that describes the group's decision and recounts how it evolved.

Much of the advantage of automated decision conferences derives from structuring the problem and modeling the decision using the microcomputer in concert with the large-screen projection capacity. Participants engage in a discussion of the strengths and weaknesses of proposed solutions; various problem areas are identified and debated; and modifications are made. This process allows fairly elaborate sensitivity analyses to check whether the assessments of the various options under consideration can withstand changes in the group's working assumptions. On the second day of a two-day conference, final refinements of the decision model occur. Having been given an opportunity to review their first efforts overnight, participants frequently discover missing variables and raise questions about assigned priorities and previously undiscussed issues related to the uncertainty of the decision environment. They are actively encouraged to look for better alternatives, to bring their assumptions to the surface, and to raise various "what if" questions. The microcomputer and software support allow for rapid revisions and updating of proposed solutions.

GDSS versus gdss

At an international conference on decision making, Huber (1982b) reminded us of a fairly well-known but often overlooked fact: Every administrator possesses and uses a decision support system (dss) that contains a set of procedures for exploring possible implications and contingencies of alternative courses of action. This dss might include policy manuals, administrative guidelines, established political precautions, previous institutional procedures, personal recollections, and advice from trusted colleagues. Every administrator relies on this dss when trying to answer "what if" questions. A Decision Support System (DSS) would be that portion of decision support system (dss) that is computerized, that is, that contains computer-retrievable and manipulable models, algorithms, or equations.

In a discussion of Huber's treatment of DSS and dss, Mintzberg (1982) applauded the distinction and likened it to a similar commentary by Shapero (1977), who had caustically contrasted MANAGEMENT with management, defining the former as what various techniques propose and the latter as what managers actually do. As a partial solution for some of his concerns about the potential dangers of DSS, Mintzberg (1982, p. 282) proposed a movement toward thinking about dss. "By this I mean decoupling the system from the computer—in simple terms, building managerial support systems around clever analysts instead of fancy hardware. This, of course, is how operations research began. Maybe the DSS people, with their managerial orientation, can rediscover what operations research seems to have lost."

As Mintzberg (1982) suggested, there is a need for group decision support systems (gdss) that consider the special political and consensual nature of strategic decisions made by groups and do not overemphasize the role of elaborate hardware and software. Early attempts at Group Decision Support Systems (GDSS) generally focused on increased efficiency in retrieving, summarizing, displaying, and manipulating information, as well as the provision of heuristic models to aid the limited cognitive ability of multiple decision makers to facilitate complex calculations required in decision situations. Such GDSS primarily address only the rational and empirical objectives of strategic decision making and appear to be based primarily in the information and decision sciences.

A more recent strain of gdss concerns itself with issues of participation and involvement in strategic decision making: how to deal with conflict generated in group decision-making situations, and how to build legitimate support and conscientious commitment to a proposed solution. These systems are primarily concerned with the behavioral aspects of strategic decision making, that is, describing the sociopsychological processes of individuals and groups engaged in "political" choice making and introducing techniques to facilitate group interaction in order to achieve more consensual decisions. There is a need for development of gdss that can integrate the regulated analytical and adaptive behavioral aspects of strategic decision making. A statement by Pondy supports such an assertion: "To be *exclusively rational* is to mediate all one's perceptions and actions through a previously articulated frame of reference; to be *exclusively intuitive* is to relate to the work without the mediation of such a frame; to join rationality and intuition is to create meaningful frames of reference in the midst of acting, over time, out of one's own lived experience" (1983, p. 190).

Summary

This survey has attempted to make clear the important distinctions between tactical and strategic decision making and the related consequences for decision support systems. It has focused on group decision support systems, since much of strategic decision making involves the use of approaches that are responsive to political and consensual concerns. This review of various forms of computer-supported conference rooms has advocated that particular attention be paid to decision conferencing, for the reasons cited above. However, whether decision conferencing or some other form of computer-supported conference room is used, the development of group decision support systems is essential in dealing with four basic questions related to strategic decision making (Milter and Rohrbaugh, 1985):

What Organization Problem Should Be Solved? Elegant solutions are useless if they solve the wrong problem. Because most institutional problems are never fully diagnosed, the effectiveness of strategic decision making depends on a continuing and adaptive process, including learning more both about difficulties encountered and about others' perceptions of what should be done.

Which Decision Model Should Be Used? Selecting a decision model is a meta-decision problem (that is, a problem about how to solve a problem) that requires administrators to recognize the appropriate match between the characteristics of their diagnosis of the problem and the features of the various decision processes that might be used. Often, the selection of a decision model is not so much a function of the intrinsic attributes of a problem as of the decision makers themselves.

How Should the Decision Structure Be Defined? Selecting a decision model is only the first part of the decision structuring process. Constructing the complete decision framework is subject to many cognitive biases and limitations that decision support systems, if thoughtfully designed, can ameliorate. There is no software available that can assure an adequate decision structure; its "goodness" depends on the combined skills of GDSS builders and users.

Who Should Be Involved in Making the Choice? Strategic decision making requires the participation of every individual with a significant stake in the solution. Strategic decision making is fundamentally a group process, with all the attendant political and consensual problems. It is in response to these obvious questions about collective decision-making processes that group decision support systems are being developed.

References

DeSanctis, G., and Gallupe, B. "Group Decision Support Systems: A New Frontier." *Data Base,* 1985, *16,* 3–10.

Drucker, P. F. *The Practice of Management.* New York: Harper & Row, 1954.

Harrison, E. F. *The Managerial Decision-Making Process.* (2nd ed.). Boston: Houghton Mifflin, 1981.

Hogue, J. T., and Watson, J. T. "An Examination of Decision Makers' Utilization of Decision Support System Output." *Information and Management,* 1985, *8,* 205–212.

Huber, G. P. "Group Decision Support Systems as Aids in the Use of Structured Group Management Techniques." *Transactions of the Second International Conference on Decision Support Systems,* San Francisco, 1982a, 96–108.

Huber, G. P. "Decision Support Systems: Their Present Nature and Future Limitations." In G. R. Ungson and D. N. Braunstein (Eds.), *Decision Making: An Interdisciplinary Inquiry.* Boston: Kent, 1982b.

Huber, G. P. "Issues on the Design of Group Decision Support Systems." *MIS Quarterly,* 1984, *8,* 195–204.

Keen, P. G. W. "Decision Support Systems: A Research Perspective." In G. Fick and R. H. Sprague (Eds.), *Decision Support Systems: Issues and Challenges.* New York: Pergamon, 1980.

Keen, P. G. W., and Scott Morton, M. S. *Decision Support Systems: An Organizational Perspective.* Reading, Mass.: Addison-Wesley, 1978.

Kraemer, K. L., and King, J. L. *Computer Supported Conference Rooms: Final Report of a State of the Art Study.* Unpublished report, University of California at Irvine, 1983.

Milter, R. G., and Rohrbaugh, J. "Microcomputers and Strategic Decision Making." *Public Productivity Review,* 1986, *9* (2–3), 175–189.

Mintzberg, H. "Comments on the Huber, Kunreuther and Schoemaker, and Chestnut and Jacoby Papers." In G. R. Ungson and D. N. Braunstein (Eds.), *Decision Making: An Interdisciplinary Inquiry.* Boston: Kent, 1982.

Phillips, L. D. "Decision Support for Managers." In H. J. Otway and M. Peltu (Eds.), *The Managerial Challenge of New Office Technology.* Boston: Butterworthe, 1984.

Pondy, L. R. "Union of Rationality and Intuition in Management Action." In. S. Srivastra (Ed.), *The Executive Mind.* San Francisco: Jossey-Bass, 1983.

Quinn, R. E., Rohrbaugh, J., and McGrath, M. R. "Automated Decision Conferencing: How it Works." *Personnel,* 1985, *21,* 49–55.

Shapero, A. "What MANAGEMENT Says and What Managers Do." *Interfaces,* 1977, 106–108.

Simon, H. A. "A Behavioral Model of Rational Choice." In H. A. Simon (Ed.), *Models of Man: Social and Rational.* New York: Wiley, 1957.

Simon, H. A. *The New Science of Management Decision.* New York: Harper & Row, 1960.

Michael Robert McGrath is assistant professor of management and organization in the School of Business Administration at the University of Southern California.

A powerful yet straightforward computer-based approach to university resource allocation has been successfully integrated with group process techniques to assist top-level administrators in making difficult choices.

Resource Allocation Models and the Budgeting Process

Richard G. Milter

There has been much debate over the introduction of computers into the arena where key strategic choices are made. Techniques developed to facilitate strategic decision processes, such as consensus mapping (Hart and others, 1985), strategic assumption surfacing (Mitroff and Emshoff, 1979), strategic issue management (Ansoff, 1980), program planning (Delbecq and others, 1975), and strategic issues diagnosis (Dutton and others, 1983), are a few of the many approaches that do not rely on computer assistance. Due to the "messy" nature of strategic decisions (Ackoff, 1974) and the fact that they typically involve more than one person (Mitroff and Emshoff, 1979), it is thought wise to be wary of using conventional computer-based techniques that may force an unrealistic simplification of the problem (Hart and others, 1985), conflict with the learning and problem-solving styles of those involved (Geurts and others, 1986), or exclude important political considerations. The complexity of strategic problems is such that purely empirical and rational approaches to their resolution often seem incomplete in the scope of analysis and likely to result in unsatisfactory outcomes.

On the other hand, an approach to strategic problems that is dominated by subjective beliefs and ignores available information is likely to be equally inadequate. Due to the ambiguous and ill-structured nature of

J. Rohrbaugh, A. T. McCartt (Eds.). *Applying Decision Support Systems in Higher Education.* New Directions for Institutional Research, no. 49. San Francisco: Jossey-Bass, March 1986.

strategic problems (Dutton and others, 1983), intuition alone may "feel right" in the short run but may later lead to considerable regret over the chosen course of action. What is needed are decision aids that can capitalize on the ability of computers to process information with great efficiency and consistency so as to enhance, rather than limit, the creativity, judgment, and political wisdom of administrators. Such aids are available (Bonczek and others, 1979; Huber, 1982; Kull, 1982). Group Decision Support Systems (GDSS) have "increased the effectiveness of decision groups by facilitating the interactive sharing and use of information among group members" (Huber, 1984, p. 196).

Resource Allocation Models

It has been suggested that the effectiveness of GDSS can be assessed by the frequency of their use and the range of their capabilities (Huber, 1984). One of the most widely used and versatile applications of GDSS for supporting strategic decision making has involved the use of resource allocation models. Originally developed at Decisions and Designs, Inc. (Ring, 1980), resource allocation models are now in rather wide use for GDSS. Phillips (1985) has described their use in decision conferences in Great Britain; Milter and Rohrbaugh (1985) similarly report a series of applications in the United States. The analytic framework of resource allocation models is simple, yet it leads to dramatic insights and creative solutions in the context of decision conferences.

Variables and Levels. The basic building block of a resource allocation model is called a *variable*. It is defined as an item that competes with other items for the same scarce resource—for example, money, time, or space. Such items are called variables because the amount of the resource that could be invested on any one item is not fixed and could be traded off against investments on other items. Each of these variables competing for the same resource is defined further by two or more specific "levels" of potential investment associated with ever-increasing commitments of the resource.

As a simple example, suppose several decision makers are interested in making the best possible use of funds to purchase a microcomputer system with three components: random access memory (RAM), input devices, and a printer. These components are considered variables because varying amounts of money (the scarce resource) could be invested in each. Each variable is described by increasingly attractive levels of resource commitment: RAM is described in terms of expanding levels of memory (64K, 128K, 256K, 512K); the levels of input devices are a built-in keyboard, a separate keyboard, a separate keyboard with a numeric pad, a separate keyboard with a numeric pad and a mouse, and a separate keyboard with a numeric pad, mouse, and light pen; and printer levels include dot matrix, dot matrix with near-letter quality, or dot matrix with near-letter quality and color graphics.

Costs, Benefits, and Relative Weights. Each level within a variable is described in terms of its cost and its benefit relative to the other levels. Costs are assessed in the units by which the resource is measured (for example, time in weeks or space in square yards). Benefit scores represent judgments about the strategic advantage of increasing one's investment from one level to the next within a variable. The lowest and highest levels are typically set at 0 and 100, respectively.

To continue the example, the lowest level of RAM (64K) is assigned a benefit value of 0. This does not imply that no strategic advantage is derived from this level of investment, but rather that 64K provides the least benefit of any investment contemplated for the variable RAM. The highest level of RAM (512K) is assigned the benefit value of 100, and intermediary levels of memory capacity (as well as those of input devices and printer) are placed in relative positions on this benefit scale. The cost of each level of hardware investment (in dollars) is also assessed for each level of the three variables.

Finally, relative weights are assigned to each variable to reflect the comparative advantage to be achieved by increasing from the lowest to the highest investment level in one variable relative to similar possible increases in investments in the levels of the other variables. In this example, the advantage of a full investment in the highest level of RAM (relative weight of 30) is judged three times as beneficial as adding near-letter quality and color graphics to a dot-matrix printer. (The smallest weight is arbitrarily set at 10.) The most important shift in investment is in input devices (4.5 times as beneficial as the contemplated increase in printer investment).

When the variables and levels have been defined and the costs, benefits, and relative weights assigned, the model structure is complete. Figure 1 provides a summary of the model for the example described above.

Investment Progression and Efficient Frontier. Once judgments have been made about costs, benefits, and relative weights, it is possible to calculate the benefit-cost ratios associated with an increased investment in any variable in the resource allocation model. In order to compute these ratios, the benefit values are first multiplied by the relative weight for each variable. The weighted benefit value of the lower level is then subtracted from the weighted benefit value of the next higher level. Dividing this difference in the weighted benefit values by the difference in the respective costs of the two levels produces each specific benefit-cost ratio. The computational formula is as follows:

$$\frac{WiBi,_{j+1} - WiBi,_{j}}{Ci,_{j+1} - Ci,_{j}}$$

Figure 1. Sample Model Structure

```
------------------------------------------------------------------
 1    RANDOM ACCESS MEMORY    Weight     30

Level   1:  64K                        Cost     400.00    Benefit     0
Level   2:  128K                       Cost     750.00    Benefit    50
Level   3:  256K                       Cost    1200.00    Benefit    75
Level   4:  512K                       Cost    4000.00    Benefit   100


------------------------------------------------------------------
 2    INPUT DEVICES           Weight     45

Level   1:  Built-in Keyboard          Cost     200.00    Benefit     0
Level   2:  Separate Keyboard          Cost     300.00    Benefit    50
Level   3:  + Numeric Pad              Cost     375.00    Benefit    75
Level   4:  + Mouse                    Cost     500.00    Benefit    90
Level   5:  + Light Pen                Cost     750.00    Benefit   100


------------------------------------------------------------------
 3    PRINTER                 Weight     10

Level   1:  Dot Matrix                 Cost     200.00    Benefit     0
Level   2:  + Near-Letter-Quality      Cost     350.00    Benefit    75
Level   3:  + Color Graphics           Cost     800.00    Benefit   100
```

where Wi is the relative weight of the ith variable, Bi,j is the benefit value of the jth level of the ith variable, and Ci,j is the amount of the resource required for the jth level of the ith variable.

It is the ordering of these ratios that highlights what incremental investments in the model will be most beneficial relative to the costs incurred. The ranking of levels from "most return" to "least return" on investment is called the *investment progression,* while the graphic display of the cumulative benefits and costs associated with this progression is known as the *efficient frontier.*

Advantages of the Method. The model provides a useful structure for complex allocation problems involving scarce resources. Quantitative and qualitative judgments about the elements of the problem are made at each step of the modeling process. When the model is developed by a group of decision makers having access to a microcomputer, they are able

- To display and update group judgments about the costs and benefits of each investment level contemplated in the model
- To compute the optimal investment progression generated by the ordering of benefit-cost ratios implied by the model, as well as the efficient frontier of ever-increasing resource investments
- To identify the specific level of investment on every variable that would produce the most return for any specified amount of total resource expenditure contemplated.

As the decision makers review and evaluate the implications of the way in which they have structured the problem and assessed the costs and benefits of different courses of action, consideration of new variables and levels is often stimulated. As refinement of the model continues, the group of decision makers are able

- To compare the relative overall cost and benefit of any proposed allocation of resources with other contemplated allocations
- To compare any proposed allocation of resources with more efficient ones that either cost less while providing the same overall benefit or provide more benefit while costing no more
- To perform sensitivity analyses by modifying the group judgments of the benefits and costs and then observing any changes in the allocation of resources that such reassessments imply.

The resource allocation model provides a group with a common framework within which to view a strategic problem and a common vocabulary with which to discuss relevant considerations. Final decisions, therefore, are more likely to be based on a mutual understanding of realistic options and to produce consensus. Furthermore, the model ensures that any decision is not based solely on data contained in a computer-based information system. An essential element of model building is the elicitation of group judgment involving participants' beliefs, attitudes, and values. The users of any model must be able to understand its function or else they will be skeptical of the decision support it provides (Steiner, 1979, p. 251). When confronting a complex strategic problem, decision makers cannot be expected to rely on a "black box" to tell them what steps should be taken. The resource allocation model provides an elegantly simple method that can be easily understood, yet it also offers the opportunity for extensive and sophisticated testing of multiple allocation strategies. The remainder of this chapter discusses its application to a most critical strategic problem faced by administrators in higher education: the budgeting process.

Budgeting in Higher Education

One of the most pressing strategic concerns facing administrators in higher education today is how to allocate resources in a way that best achieves an institution's goals and priorities. A resource allocation problem is "strategic" in the sense that it involves a set of decisions which is typically unstructured, complex, and open-ended (Mintzberg and others, 1976). The elements of the decision process are interdependent (Mitroff and Emshoff, 1979), and decision making becomes a "critical tool for achieving important organizational changes" (Chaffee, 1983, p. 402). Nevertheless, it is virtually impossible for administrators to use to the fullest all available relevant information and to assess every internal and external organizational need. Even if all such information were to be incorporated into the budgeting process, competing priorities would make difficult a final allocation of scarce resources that would satisfy all those in the institution who have a stake in the outcome. Given the complexity of the institutional environment and the trend toward declining resources, university administrators typically try to rationalize the process by developing explicit and objective criteria for their budgetary decisions (Cameron and Whetten, 1983; Rubin, 1977; Whetten, 1981).

Political versus Rational Approaches. While several studies found the use of objective criteria to be the primary factor that influences the budgeting process in higher education (Chaffee, 1983; Rubin, 1980; Cameron, 1983), other research has identified situations in which budgetary decisions were based on the relative power of the parties involved (Pfeffer and Salancik, 1974; Pfeffer and Moore, 1980). The perspective that views power as a key element in the budgeting process emphasizes the role of academic departments as *resource recipients.* Studies supporting this perspective have sought to understand why politically-based departmental power overshadows administrative authority as a primary factor. Schick (1985) has presented the "administrator as resource allocator" in his recent study of decision-making behavior in universities facing conditions of reduced resources. The degree to which rationality or political power plays a role in university budgeting decisions has been linked to the amount of resources available and the openness of the budget process, but research in this area has produced contradictory results. Some research concludes that when resources are scarce departmental power becomes the key consideration in budgetary decisions (Pfeffer and Moore, 1980). Other research has found greater use of objective criteria as resources become scarce (Cameron, 1983).

Convergence of Both Approaches. Although certain highly structured models for decision making may be socially or psychologically naive (Geurts and others, 1986), it will often be in the best interests of administrators to systematize the process to some extent. In fact, regardless of whether a rational process produces better decisions, it is likely to be more comfortable, more acceptable, and less contentious for an organization like a major research university than any other process (Chaffee, 1983, p. 402). The budgeting process most appropriate for a college or university, however, may not conform entirely to either the rational or political power perspective. A more eclectic process may be closer to reality in most institutional budgeting cases (Chaffee, 1983), as administrators strive to make budgetary decisions in a systematic, consistent, and fair manner while balancing the political considerations inherent in any strategic decision.

Case in Point: A University Budgeting Process

A large public university experiencing a scarcity of resources provides an ideal setting for building GDSS. Although the accounts presented in this chapter are real, the exact names and labels have been changed to protect the confidentiality of the process. Once a year, top administrators at the university meet to allocate resources for equipment, temporary services, and supplies and expenses (S & E) for the coming fiscal year. Requests for financial support to cover proposed projects in these areas come from six university divisions (the president's office, academic affairs, finance and business, research and educational development, university affairs, and student affairs). Since the university has limited resources available to cover equipment, temporary service, and S & E needs, the allocation of funds among the various budget requests is a problem of clarifying organizational priorities.

The problem has become more acute during recent periods of severe resource scarcity. Once the budget is established, funds cannot be interchanged between the three budget categories. As the final budget decisions are made, therefore, administrators face a number of difficult choices. What configuration of temporary service allocations provides the most benefit to the university at the cost level currently available? Are certain S & E requests too expensive for the benefit level they provide? If money is needed from the equipment pool to cover immediate university needs in other areas, what equipment purchases should be the first to be cancelled?

Although several important decisions about the equipment, temporary services, and S & E budgets have already been made by university administrators as the deadline for submission of final budget requests approaches, many questions remain unresolved. Seeking a coherent approach that would lead to more widely acceptable allocation of resources and full commitment to the budget decisions, top administrators have worked together since 1982 using a resource allocation model as part of a larger design for GDSS, developed in collaboration with the university's decision support unit.

Preliminary Problem Structuring. Prior to an annual decision conference involving the university president and five vice presidents, a member of the university's decision support unit meets individually with each vice president. The purpose of these preliminary sessions is to establish the structure of the resource allocation models that will be used to assist in making final budget decisions. Three model structures are developed by the vice presidents to make explicit the needs of their divisions for additional resources in equipment, temporary services, and S & E. Because many of the budget items are fixed costs and have already been committed through standing obligations, the items dealt with by the vice presidents in these models are truly discretionary and assume tremendous importance (Chaffee, 1983, p. 402). Although the amount of money to be allocated in these discretionary budget sessions is relatively small with respect to the total university operating budget, their allocation involves administrative judgment and leadership. They represent the last chance to direct resources so as to develop new objectives or enhance continuing projects for the coming fiscal year.

The vice presidents independently develop their divisions' variables and levels into individual models for each of the three budget areas. They then assign costs and benefits to every level of each variable in their models. In this application, the lowest level of every variable is defined as "none," that is, no additional investment in the proposed item. Relative weights are also set to reflect priorities—the relative benefit of one set of investments with respect to another. For simple structures (models with few variables), this task is rather straightforward, with the vice presidents directly placing relative weights on the variables. In more complex models, the decision support unit member asks the vice presidents to make a series of comparisons of pairs of variables as a way of identifying priorities. These preferences are then checked for consistency and used to establish the set of relative weights to be reviewed at the decision conference.

An initial decision model is generated for each budget area, complete with variables, levels, costs, benefits, and relative weights. For purposes of organization, each variable is arbitrarily given a number. In this example, variables numbered 3, 8, 9, 10, 11, 12, and 15 are shown in Figure 2, which displays a portion of the total model for one university division, as designed by its vice president. In this example, variable number 12, "interdisciplinary program development," contains six levels. The first level, "none," is to do nothing additional in this area and, therefore, involves no additional cost. (Because these models reflect discretionary resources, there could already be an allocation in the base budget.) The benefit value of the initial level is set at 0. The second level within this variable, "teacher education" (more precisely, some interdisciplinary program development activity *within* the teacher education department of the university), will cost $1000 and is valued by the vice president at 30 on the benefit scale—that is, 30% of the strategic advantage of full investment in program development up to and including level 6 ($5000).

The third level adds some interdisciplinary program development in the "health policy" area, costs an additional $1000, and is worth twenty-five more units of benefit, according to the vice president. In contrast, the move in investment from the fifth to the sixth level adds "computer assisted instruction & physics," also at a cost of $1000, yet only increases the total benefit of this variable by ten units. The benefit value is typically greater for the preferred first levels of investment than it is for subsequent ones.

The variable "interdisciplinary program development" was assigned a relative weight of 70 in comparison to all of the other variables in the model. The first variable displayed in Figure 2, "expand CDHP activity," was given a relative weight of 50. This means that the strategic advantage in moving from the initial level ("none") to the final level ("proposed expansion") in this variable is less valuable than moving through all the levels within the variable "interdisciplinary program development." The latter is thought to be 1.4 times as valuable as the former. With relative weights of 100, achieving all levels in each of the variables "faculty recruitment," "graduate recruitment publications," and "graduate recruitment follow-up," is estimated to be twice as valuable as gaining all levels in the variable "expand CDHP activity." The strategic advantage of adding "proposed coverage" in the variable "institute membership" is assessed as equal to that gained by adding all six levels in the variable "interdisciplinary program development." Of slightly more benefit than that derived from achieving all levels in the variables "interdisciplinary program development" or "institute membership" is the value of adding the "proposed coverage" of "maintenance for microcomputers" (with a relative weight of 80).

When the benefit-cost ratios for every contemplated investment in the model have been calculated and ranked in order of "return," the investment progression is available for vice-presidential review. The portion of the resource allocation model shown in Figure 2 yields a portion of the investment progression presented in Figure 3. The first investment displayed is number 11 (out of a total of twenty-seven investments in this model's progression). This investment recommends that the variable "graduate recruitment follow-up" be given the resources to move from level 2

Figure 2. Model Structure

```
-----------------------------------------------------------------
 3   EXPAND  CDHP  ACTIVITY               Weight      50

Level  1: None                     Cost        0.00   Benefit    0
Level  2: Partial Expansion        Cost     1000.00   Benefit   70
Level  3: Proposed Expansion       Cost     2500.00   Benefit  100


-----------------------------------------------------------------
 8   MAINTENANCE  FOR  MICRO              Weight      80

Level  1: None                     Cost        0.00   Benefit    0
Level  2: Proposed Coverage        Cost     7100.00   Benefit  100
-----------------------------------------------------------------
 9   FACULTY  RECRUITMENT                 Weight     100

Level  1: None                     Cost        0.00   Benefit    0
Level  2: One                      Cost     2000.00   Benefit   30
Level  3: Two                      Cost     4000.00   Benefit   55
Level  4: Three                    Cost     6000.00   Benefit   75
Level  5: Four                     Cost     8000.00   Benefit   90
Level  6: Five                     Cost    10000.00   Benefit  100


-----------------------------------------------------------------
 10   GRAD  RECRUIT  PUBLICA               Weight     100

Level  1: None                     Cost        0.00   Benefit    0
Level  2: Some Publications        Cost     5000.00   Benefit   80
Level  3: Proposed Publication     Cost     7400.00   Benefit  100


-----------------------------------------------------------------
 11   GRAD  RECRT  FOLLOW-UP               Weight     100

Level  1: None                     Cost        0.00   Benefit    0
Level  2: Partial Follow-up        Cost     1500.00   Benefit   60
Level  3: Proposed Follow-up       Cost     2500.00   Benefit  100


-----------------------------------------------------------------
 12   INTERDISC  PROG  DEV                 Weight      70

Level  1: None                     Cost        0.00   Benefit    0
Level  2: Teacher Education        Cost     1000.00   Benefit   30
Level  3: + Health Policy          Cost     2000.00   Benefit   55
Level  4: + Archives               Cost     3000.00   Benefit   75
Level  5: + Dispute Management     Cost     4000.00   Benefit   90
Level  6: + CAI & Physics          Cost     5000.00   Benefit  100
-----------------------------------------------------------------
 15   INSTITUTE  MEMBERSHIP                Weight      70

Level  1: None                     Cost        0.00   Benefit    0
Level  2: Proposed Membership      Cost      500.00   Benefit  100
```

("partial follow-up") to level 3 ("proposed follow-up"). Such an addition to the model brings the total cost to $14,000 at a return of 61.8% of the total benefit obtainable by funding every variable at its highest level. The next investment, number 12, recommends that "partial expansion" be funded in order to begin to "expand CDHP activity," which costs an additional $1000 and brings the accumulated benefit to 64.6% of the total. The next most beneficial investment in the figure displayed is to fund "interdisciplinary program development" in "teacher education," followed by "interdisciplinary program development" in "health policy," covering the "proposed" level for "research clusters," adding "some publications" for "graduate recruitment," supporting "one faculty recruitment," funding "archives" in "interdisciplinary program development," supporting another "faculty recruitment," and covering the "proposed" level of "maintenance for microcomputers." The final investment displayed brings the total cost to $38,100 at a return of 92.1% of the total possible benefit.

Each incremental investment offering the next best "return" (as reflected in its benefit-cost ratio) corresponds to a specific point on the efficient frontier, as shown in Figure 4. Investments are added incrementally until all the levels in all the variables in the model have been included (although their benefit-cost ratios may be quite small). The efficient frontier indicates that the benefit-cost ratios are relatively high through the first investments up to about $125,000. Thereafter, the marginal return on investment decreases, requiring an additional $375,000 to provide the remaining 50% of the total benefit.

After a careful review of the model structures, efficient frontiers, and investment progressions, a vice president may wish to make refinements in a model to bring certain variables or levels into the investment progression at an earlier or later point in the sequence. Such adjustments are handled easily by the decision support unit member, using a microcomputer. Once the models are thought to reflect the funding requests of each vice president appropriately, they are ready for consideration at the annual decision conference.

The Decision Conference. The major contribution of the decision support unit to the budgeting process is provided in the context of a decision conference. In addition to the five vice presidents, participants in the decision conference include the president and two staff members from the university's financial management office. The decision support unit provides four individuals who facilitate the decision process, work with the microcomputer, record the rationale behind the decisions reached, and prepare the conference report. The conference room is equipped with a large, round conference table, several white boards, and a large display screen that allows immediate inspection of the implications of various allocation strategies as graphically displayed by the microcomputer.

The first group task involves the integration of the individual mod-

Figure 3. Investment Progression

```
INVESTMENT 11

Variable   11:GRAD RECRT FOLLOW-UP

   Level   2:Partial Follow-up
    to
   Level   3:Proposed Follow-up

COST   14000.0   BENEFIT   61.8


INVESTMENT 12

Variable    3:EXPAND CDHP ACTIVITY

   Level   1:None
    to
   Level   2:Partial Expansion

COST   15000.0   BENEFIT   64.6


INVESTMENT 13

Variable   12:INTERDISC PROG DEV

   Level   1:None
    to
   Level   2:Teacher Education

COST   16000.0   BENEFIT   66.3


INVESTMENT 14

Variable   12:INTERDISC PROG DEV

   Level   2:Teacher Education
    to
   Level   3:+ Health Policy

COST   17000.0   BENEFIT   67.8


INVESTMENT 15

Variable   14:RESEARCH CLUSTERS

   Level   1:None
    to
   Level   2:Proposed Clusters

COST   21000.0   BENEFIT   73.5


INVESTMENT 16

Variable   10:GRAD RECRUIT PUBLICA

   Level   1:None
    to
   Level   2:Some Publications

COST   26000.0   BENEFIT   80.0


INVESTMENT 17

Variable    9:FACULTY RECRUITMENT

   Level   1:None
    to
   Level   2:One

COST   28000.0   BENEFIT   82.4


INVESTMENT 18

Variable   12:INTERDISC PROG DEV

   Level   3:+ Health Policy
    to
   Level   4:+ Archives

COST   29000.0   BENEFIT   83.5


INVESTMENT 19

Variable    9:FACULTY RECRUITMENT

   Level   2:One
    to
   Level   3:Two

COST   31000.0   BENEFIT   85.6


INVESTMENT 20

Variable    8:MAINTENANCE FOR MICRO

   Level   1:None
    to
   Level   2:Proposed Coverage

COST   38100.0   BENEFIT   92.1
```

Figure 4. Efficient Frontier

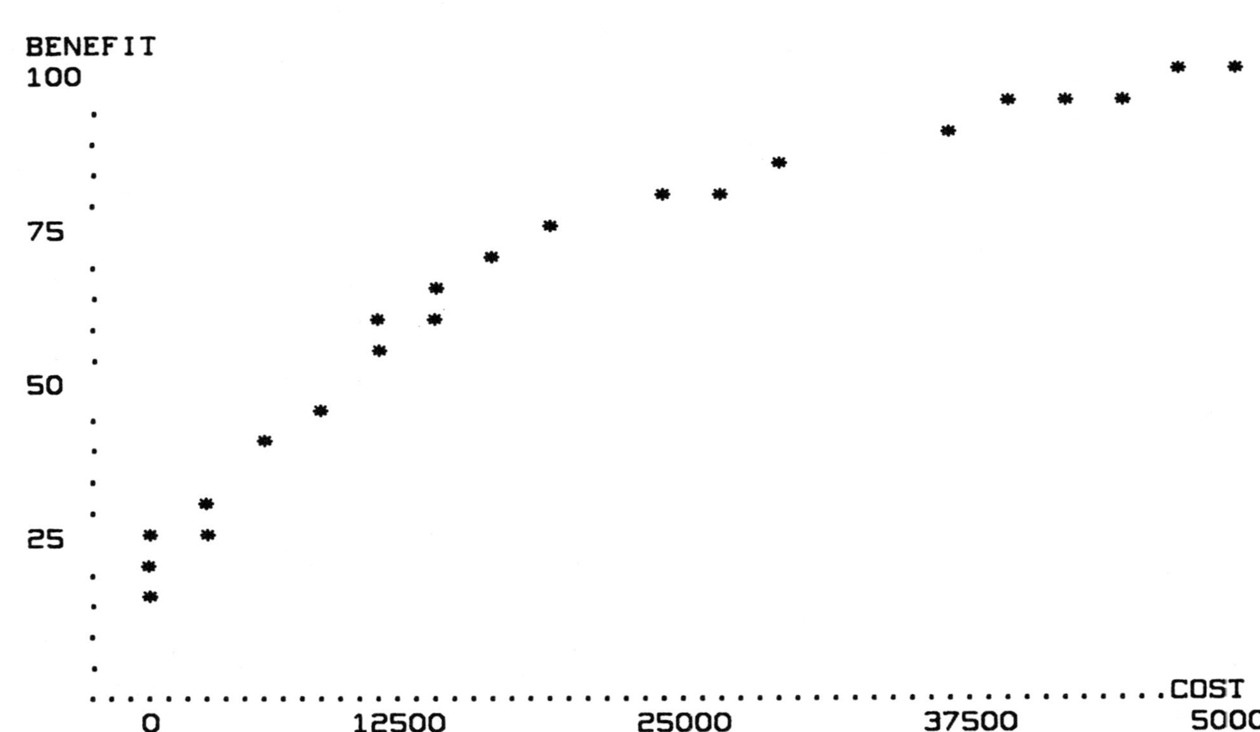

els developed by each vice president into one composite model that represents university-wide goals and priorities. The merging of the five models (one from each of the vice presidents) for each of the three budget areas (equipment, temporary services, and S & E) is accomplished analytically, as a result of a series of group judgments. One proposed investment is selected systematically from the investment progression of each vice president. (The incremental benefit of the investment is known to the vice president and decision support unit but not to the rest of the group.) These five items are listed side by side on a white board, and conference participants must arrange them on a scale of 0 (least university-wide benefit) to 100 (most university-wide benefit). Such comparisons are repeated five to seven times until a stable estimate can be made of the relative importance of the five investment progressions to university-wide objectives.

Following the group's convergence on the relative weights for the five vice presidential models, an initial university model is generated by adjusting the benefit-cost ratios with the weights derived from the group comparisons and then ordering these new ratios from all five lists into a single investment progression. This calculation is completed on the microcomputer in less than a minute of conference time. The activities above are performed at the decision conference for each of the three budget areas (equipment, temporary services, and S & E). The group then takes each budget area in turn and carefully inspects the proposed investment progression, turning its energy toward achieving consensus regarding the precise ordering of items listed in the investment progression. Refinements are made in the model when the group believes specific items should be given greater strategic advantage and thus entered earlier into the progression. Of special interest are those items that appear near the cutoff points determined by available resources. The group works toward agreement that those items listed in the progression prior to depleting present resources are the ones that should be funded. If more resources should become available, those items immediately following the cutoff point would receive support. If resources become more scarce than anticipated, the items appearing nearest to the cutoff point in the progression would be the first to lose funding.

Report for Administrators. Before the administrators leave the conference room, each is presented with a printout documenting the activities of the conference and rationale for the budgetary decisions that were made. This document includes the charts and graphs of the model structure, the investment progressions, and the efficient frontiers. If changes in cost estimates or model assumptions are made following the completion of conference activities, such modifications are easily incorporated into the model, and updated copies of the reports are distributed.

Conclusion

Reaching a consensus on the priority of items submitted for funding is a difficult task. During times of decreasing resources, the process tends to become even more conflict-ridden, as individuals seek new ways to protect their organizational turf. After being involved in the approach described above, however, one administrator wrote, in an unsolicited letter, "I am convinced we spent the available resources to their optimal effectiveness and efficiency. More than that, the entire decision-making group came away committed to the expenditures that we agreed upon. It is rare that you are able to do both of those things."

The GDSS approach followed at the university incorporates the perspectives of both the rational and political models of budgeting. One of the benefits of the approach is that the amount of time devoted to a problem can be substantially reduced, because the discussion of the issues proceeds in a systematic, highly focused manner. In this example, the initial sessions require that each vice president meet with a decision support unit member for one or two hours. In 1982, the time required for completion of the decision conference totaled ten hours. As the GDSS has evolved over time, skepticism about the approach has dissipated, and participants have increased their confidence and skill in using the model. The process has become more efficient each year, now requiring about six hours and much less direct involvement of the decision support unit.

Another way in which the university administrators have learned from the resource allocation model is reflected in their more efficient preparation for the decision conference. In structuring their initial discretionary budget items, the vice presidents have also begun to select a greater number of less expensive items and to refrain from including very costly single items. In the four years of experience with GDSS, the average dollar amount per requested item has dropped 66 percent. It appears that this trend will continue, as the vice presidents learn that larger benefit-cost ratios usually result from carefully planned, less expensive proposals for university investment. As a result, the entire university benefits, because less demanding projects push against its limited discretionary budget.

By integrating analytic techniques and open group processes, the use of GDSS at a university helps decision makers move relatively quickly toward consensus solutions. The genuine fairness of the approach facilitates commitment to the process and its outcomes. Although the approach imposes a systematic and efficient structure on the problem, subjectivity and good political judgment are highly encouraged throughout the process. The key to good decision making is not to remove subjective values but rather to ensure that the process of making strategic choices is consistent and coherent and results in a decision that accurately reflects those subjective values. Experience at this university has shown that, when strategic options are evaluated with the use of GDSS, the choices made usually reflect a mutual understanding of the organization's priorities and a thorough consideration of all relevant issues.

References

Ackoff, R. A. *Redesigning the Future.* New York: Wiley, 1974.

Ansoff, H. I. "Strategic Issue Management." *Strategic Management Journal,* 1980, *1,* 131-148.

Bonczek, R. H., Holsapple, C. W., and Whinston, A. B. "Computer-based Support of Organizational Decision Making." *Decision Sciences,* 1979, *10,* 268-291.

Cameron, K. "Strategic Responses to Conditions of Decline: Higher Education and the Private Sector." *Journal of Higher Education,* 1983, *54,* 359-380.

Cameron, K., and Whetten, D. A. "Models of the Organizational Life Cycle: Applications to Higher Education." *Review of Higher Education,* 1983, *6,* 269-290.

Chaffee, E. E. "The Role of Rationality in University Budgeting." *Research in Higher Education,* 1983, *19,* 387-406.

Delbecq, A., Van de Ven, A., and Gustafson, D. *Group Techniques for Program Planning.* Glenview, Ill.: Scott, Foresman, 1975.

Dutton, J. E., Fahey, L., and Narayanan, V. K. "Toward Understanding Strategic Issues and Diagnosis." *Strategic Management Journal,* 1983, *4,* 307-323.

Geurts, J. L. A., Hart, S. L., and Caplan, N. S. "Decision Techniques in Social Research: A Contingency Framework for Problem Solving." *Human Systems Management,* 1986, *5* (4), 333-347.

Hart, S., Boroush, M., Enk, G., and Hornick, W. "Managing Complexity Through Consensus Mapping: Technology for the Structuring of Group Decisions." *Academy of Management Review,* 1985, *10* (3), 587-600.

Hills, F. S. and Mahoney, T. A. "University Budgets and Organizational Decision Making." *Administrative Science Quarterly,* 1978, *23,* 454-465.

Huber, G. P. "Group Decision Support Systems as Aids in the Use of Structured Group Management Techniques." *Transactions of the Second International Conference on Decision Support Systems,* San Francisco, June 1982.

Huber, G. P. "Issues in the Design of Group Decision Support Systems." *MIS Quarterly,* 1984, *8* (3), 195-204.

Kull, D. J. "Group Decisions: Can Computers Help?" *Computer Decisions,* May 1982, 70-84, 160.

Milter, R. G., and Rohrbaugh, J. "Microcomputers and Strategic Decision Making." *Public Productivity Review,* 1985, *9* (2-3), 175-189.

Mintzberg, H., Raisinghani, D., and Theoret, A. "The Structure of 'Unstructured' Decision Processes." *Administrative Science Quarterly,* 1976, *21,* 246-275.

Mitroff, I. I., and Emshoff, J. R. "On Strategic Assumption-Making: A Dialectical Approach to Policy and Planning." *Academy of Management Review,* 1979, *4* (1), 1-12.

Pfeffer, J., and Moore, W. L. "Power in University Budgeting: A Replication and Extension." *Administrative Science Quarterly,* 1980, *25,* 637-653.

Pfeffer, J., and Salancik, G. R. "Organizational Decision Making as a Political Process: The Case of a University Budget." *Administrative Science Quarterly,* 1974, *19,* 135-151.

Phillips, L. "Systems for Solutions." *Datamation Business,* April 1985, 26-29.

Ring, R. "A New Way to Make Decisions." *Graduate Engineer,* November 1980, 46-49.

Rubin, I. "Universities in Stress: Decision Making under Conditions of Reduced Resources." *Social Science Quarterly,* 1977, *58,* 242-254.

Rubin, I. "Retrenchment and Flexibility in Public Organizations." In C. H. Levine and I. Rubin (Eds.), *Fiscal Stress and Public Policy.* Beverly Hills, Calif.: Sage, 1980, 159-178.

Schick, A. G. "University Budgeting: Administrative Perspective, Budget Structure, and Budget Process." *Academy of Management Review,* 1985, *10* (4), 794-802.

Steiner, G. A. *Strategic Planning.* New York: Free Press, 1979.

Whetten, D. A. "Organizational Responses to Scarcity: Exploring the Obstacles to Innovative Approaches to Retrenchment in Education." *Educational Administration Quarterly,* 1981, *17,* 80-97.

Richard G. Milter is associate director of Decision Techtronics Group and a faculty member in the School of Business, State University of New York at Albany. He teaches courses in quantitative methods, behavioral management theory, leadership, and decision making.

Simulation can be used effectively to anticipate the long-term consequences of institutional policies, thus avoiding costly trial-and-error practices.

System Dynamics Models and Institutional Pricing Decisions

Fiona Chen

In an effort to help administrators and policy makers improve the quality of their judgments, management scientists have developed various simulation models that borrow heavily from tools developed in the physical sciences. One class of simulation models is the system dynamics model, developed in the mid-1950s by Jay Forrester of the Massachusetts Institute of Technology. In recent years, it has been applied more and more frequently to complex social, economic, and political problems.

The system dynamics approach makes three major assumptions in structuring a problem. First, the problem is seen as a system of elements interconnected with each other in a causal fashion. Second, the analysis of the problem involves an assessment of the changes in the system over time. Third, the system dynamics model builder assumes that a policy change in the system will affect the system's performance over time in varied and complex ways and that the change will have unintended as well as intended consequences. The building of a system dynamics model thus involves identifying the key components of the focal problem, determining how and to what extent the components are related to each other, and constructing a representation of the problem that traces the flow of

J. Rohrbaugh, A. T. McCartt (Eds.). *Applying Decision Support Systems in Higher Education.* New Directions for Institutional Research, no. 49. San Francisco: Jossey-Bass, March 1986.

cause-and-effect relationships that are believed to characterize it. The analyst usually proceeds from a detailed flow diagram of the system to a mathematical or computerized simulation. When the system dynamics model represents well the observed behavior of the system over time, policy alternatives can be tested in computer simulations to see if the system's performance would improve after implementation of the policy.

According to Roberts (1978, pp. 3–35), the system dynamics approach provides the following advantages:

1. Policy makers are required to specify an explicit and consistent formulation of the causes of the problem. As the model is built and tested, contradictory or ambiguous assumptions must be resolved, and new insights into the structure of the problem arise.

2. The likely implications of policy alternatives can be explored.

3. Unlike many analytical tools that capture the understanding of a problem at one point in time, system dynamics models are "organic and iterative."

4. Sensitivity analyses indicate to policy makers the areas where clarification will most affect the performance of the system.

5. An operating model can serve as a tool to educate other parties about the structure of the problem and the short-term and long-term effects of policy changes and different assumptions regarding the parameters.

Definition of System Dynamics Terms

Like most analytical approaches, system dynamics has a special vocabulary that embodies the key concepts. A few of the more important terms are described below.

The *system boundary* defines and encloses the system's dynamic behavior. The model of the system focuses on the growth, decline and fluctuations occurring in a number of interrelated feedback loops within the boundary. The notion of *feedback effects* is central to system dynamics. In a feedback effect, a variable is influenced by its own past behavior; an initial cause ripples through a chain of causes and effects until the initial cause becomes an indirect effect of itself. For example, an increase in a state tax rate on business leads to relocation of some businesses in other states, which produces a decrease in the tax base and tax revenues, heightening the pressure for further increases in the tax rate.

A *positive feedback loop* is one in which the elements reinforce each other, and the system continues to grow or decline. "Positive" in this context means moving (changing) in the same direction. A reduction in one element in a positive feedback loop causes a reduction in another element. Elements in a *negative feedback loop* negate or counteract one another; an increase in one element in the loop produces a reduction in another element. Because elements in a negative feedback loop negate one another, the system is contained and strives to attain a state of equilibrium or stability.

A model involves two major types of variables. *Level variables* are those elements of the system in which accumulations of resources exist. In the example of state taxes noted above, a level variable would be the tax base. That is, at a given point in time, the number of dollars accumulated in the tax base is referred to as the level for that variable. *Rate variables* indicate the rate of change occurring in the level variables. For example, the rate at which the tax base changes in a specific time period is a rate variable.

Pricing Decisions

One of the most complex sets of decisions faced by a college or university involves setting prices for the services it provides. Prices affect every aspect of institutional life, and a number of recent developments have caused institutions to be increasingly concerned with their prices. These developments include rapidly rising institutional costs, an unstable and unpredictable economy, shrinking federal funds in support of higher education, and shifts in the age distribution of the population. Most institutions must struggle to establish a tuition level that will strike an acceptable balance among various objectives. Sometimes they conflict, for they include such diverse objectives as ensuring the institution's economic viability, attracting an adequate number of students, and maintaining institutional standards in the quality of education. The complex issues involved in setting prices for education were discussed in an earlier volume in this series, entitled *Issues in Pricing Undergraduate Education* (Litten, 1984).

Part of the difficulty in setting prices arises from the fact that many of the most crucial events that unfold are beyond the control of the institution—for example, the prices set by other institutions, the institution's costs, and the state of the economy. In addition, an institution finds it difficult to predict the short-term and long-term effects of a change in tuition, since the price of tuition affects other institutional variables through a series of complex causal relationships (Karol and Ginsburg, 1980; Turcotte, 1983; Whitla, 1984).

In this chapter, a simple system dynamics model is used to represent the main internal dynamics affecting a particular institutional pricing decision—setting a tuition rate. The model is a generic one. This hypothetical institutional system illustrates how a policy-making group can better understand the short-term and long-term effects of institutional decisions relating to the pricing of tuition by applying the techniques of system dynamics.

A System Dynamics Model of Institutional Pricing

The system dynamics model has been built for a hypothetical institution. In order to keep the example simple, the system boundary includes only factors internal to the institution. External factors affecting pricing, such as the age distribution of the population or median income, have been held constant. Furthermore, only the major cause-and-effect relationships are included in the system.

Cause-and-Effect Dynamics. The system is dominated by three positive and three negative feedback loops.

Positive Feedback Loops. There are three primary positive feedback loops driving the system to grow (or decline): enrollment, revenue, and the cost of education. In these three loops, presented in Figure 1, the elements tend to reinforce each other. The enrollment feedback loop is shown in the lower portion of Figure 1. Beginning in the lower right corner, an increase in the quality of education increases the institution's reputation, which attracts more applicants, leading to a higher enrollment. The loop is completed as higher enrollment produces a larger income for the institution, more institutional support for education, and an increase in the quality of education. In the educational cost feedback loop, when institutional revenues rise and are allocated to various institutional programs,

Figure 1. Three Positive Feedback Loops

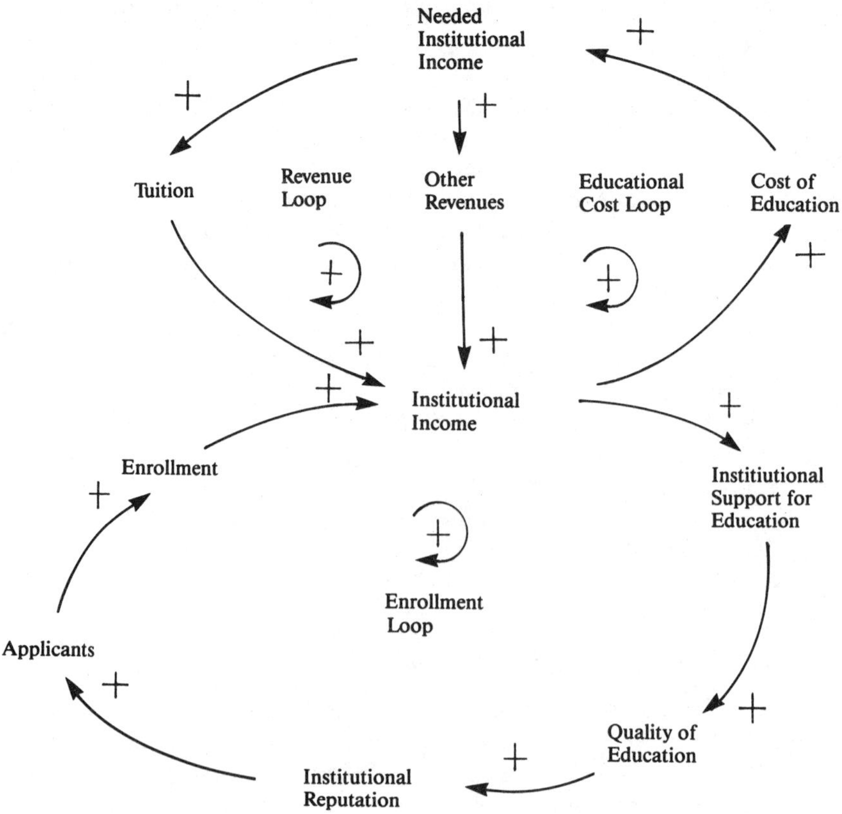

the cost of education automatically increases. Over time, this will require additional institutional income for program support. In the revenue feedback loop, the institution needs greater revenues from both tuition and non-tuition sources.

It should be stressed that a decline in one factor produces a decline in the next element in a positive feedback loop. For example, a decline in the quality of education will eventually lead to a decline in enrollment as the institution's reputation falls and fewer persons apply for admission.

Negative Feedback Loops. The system will not continue to grow (or decline) without check, however, because of three negative feedback loops: the admission standard, educational expenditure per pupil, and the inverse relationship between the tuition level and the number of applicants. As stated earlier, negative feedback loops control the system's growth, as each negative loop strives to reach a state of equilibrium.

In Figure 2, the three negative feedback loops have been added to the system. One negative loop involves the inverse relationship between the admission standard and the size of enrollment. As an institution raises its admission standard, enrollment falls. The admission standard also affects the quality of education. The system assumes that the institution's current quality of education is positively related to the admission standard. That is, the higher the quality of education, the higher the admission standard would be; and a higher admission standard presumably produces a higher quality of education. Hence, this reciprocal positive relationship introduces a fourth positive feedback loop into the system.

The chain of effects introduced by the admission standard illustrates the way in which a negative feedback loop acts to control the growth or decline of a system. Even if a higher quality of education attracts a larger and larger pool of applicants, the increase in the admission standard produced by a higher quality of education acts to maintain an equilibrium enrollment. Conversely, as quality declines, the reputation of the institution will fall, and the pool of applicants will shrink. The size of enrollment will be maintained, however, by a lower admission standard.

The negative relationship between two elements of the enrollment loop, enrollment and per-pupil educational expenditures, creates a second negative feedback loop. Although a larger enrollment raises the institution's income (given a constant tuition rate) and its support for education, an increase in the enrollment also reduces the institution's overall per-pupil expenditure, since certain program costs are fixed—not affected by the number of students. Nevertheless, lower per-pupil expenditures may well lower the quality of education. In the long run, a lower quality of education reduces the institution's reputation, the number of applicants, and enrollment.

A third negative feedback loop is formed by the inverse relationship between the tuition level and the number of applicants. Although higher

Figure 2. Complete Causal Analysis of Institutional Systems

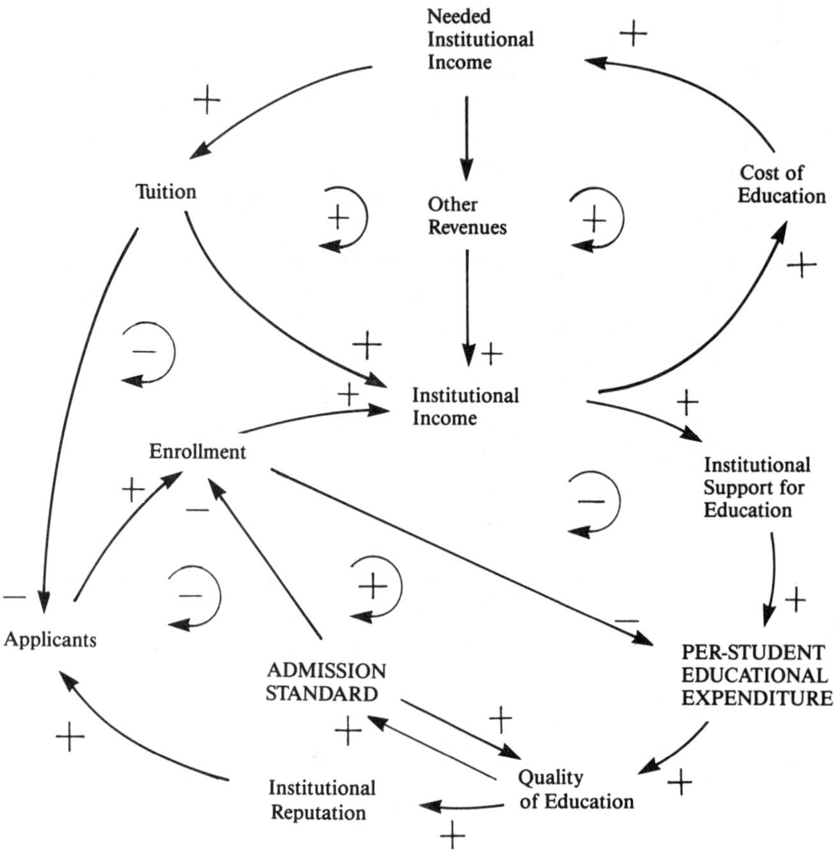

tuition increases the institution's revenues (if enrollment holds constant), it also leads to a drop in the number of applicants. This decreases enrollment (if the admission standard is held constant), and revenues fall.

To summarize this simplified model of tuition pricing, a number of forces reinforce the tendency toward continued increase or decrease in tuition. However, other institutional factors intervene to counteract this tendency.

Model Structure. The next step in building a model is to expand the pattern of relationships described above to encompass more explicit assumptions about how the system functions. The following comments summarize the assumptions incorporated into the three sectors of the model: enrollment, institutional revenue, and the quality of education.

Enrollment Sector. The number of students enrolled on a full-time basis, a level variable, is assumed to be equally affected by the number of applicants and the admission standard. The number of applicants, in turn, is influenced by changes in tuition and in the institution's reputation and by an "other" factor, which represents factors beyond the institution's control such as socioeconomic conditions.

An important concept in system dynamics is the concept of delay in transfers of information or material. It is a recognition of the fact that the consequences of many actions occur over time. A material delay involves a physical flow, such as the production or delivery of goods. Information delays are delays in perceptions or responses. For example, the time involved in gathering information is an information delay. In this model, tuition levels during the past three years form an image of the tuition level for the institution. When the present tuition differs from this historical tuition level, the number of applicants will be affected. The number of applicants is also influenced by the institution's reputation. The quality of education (a level variable) forms an institution's reputation through a long-term process. This process is somewhat different from the average tuition image, which changes more abruptly and clearly. The delay between changes in quality of education and the resulting changes in institutional reputation is much longer than the delay between changes in tuition and the alteration of the image of the tuition. Although the length of the period of delay may vary from one institution to another, this model assumes that the quality of education over the past 10 years forms the current reputation of the institution. When the current quality of education differs significantly from the institution's historical reputation, the number of applicants is influenced.

The admission standard is defined as the percentage of applicants admitted. Although this aspect of the model's structure can be varied to test different policies, in this example the standard is set at 80 percent. The admission standard is also a level variable.

Institutional Revenue Sector. The institution derives its revenues from tuition and non-tuition sources. These are both level variables in the model. Although tuition and non-tuition dollars may be affected by factors external to the institution, the institution seeks to adjust revenues internally to maintain the per-student expenditure level. The model assumes that when there is a need to adjust revenues, the institution tries to apportion the adjustment between tuition and non-tuition revenues according to their respective shares of the current total revenues. Another major assumption in this process of revenue adjustment is that the less the increase needed, the easier it is to achieve the increase. Finally, it is worth noting that tuition revenue is relatively easier for an institution to increase than non-tuition revenue.

Quality of Education Sector. The quality of education is affected by the admission standard and the per-pupil expenditure level. The per-pupil educational expenditure, a level variable, is affected by the level of institutional support for education and the size of enrollment. It is assumed that the institution does not immediately invest all of any increase in revenues in education. Only a portion of the increased revenue is committed to educational expenses. However, the institution immediately reduces its support of education when revenues decrease.

Sector Flow Diagrams. The next step in building a system dynamics model is to convert the detailed assumptions of the system into a series of flow diagrams.

Figure 3 shows the flow diagram for the institutional revenue sector. It is not necessary for the reader to understand the details of this flow diagram; the figure is presented to illustrate how the flows of information are captured graphically. The level variables are represented as a rectangular shape, and the change rate variables present a shape similar to that of a milk bottle. Dependent variables linking the level variables are known as *auxiliary variables* and are represented as circles.

Model Behavior

Testing a Scenario. The final step in building the model involves deriving a mathematical model and a computer simulation of the system. In order to illustrate the model's behavior, a hypothetical scenario was simulated. The results are shown in Figure 4. In this scenario the model starts in a state of equilibrium, in which all model variables are steady. Beginning after year two, there is a 10 percent increase each year in the number of applicants. Since the institution has established an admission standard under which 80 percent of all applicants are admitted, the number of enrollees also increases. As a result of the increased enrollment, the per-student expenditure decreases. In striving to maintain the per-pupil expenditure, the institution seeks to increase revenues. According to the model, tuition can be raised more easily than can non-tuition revenues. As a result of lower per-pupil expenditures, both the quality of education and the institution's reputation suffer over time.

Policy Testings. To illustrate further the usefulness of this model, the implications of two policy changes are explored. Once again, the time frame for the simulations is set at 10 years. Assume that in year 2 the institution begins to experience a downward trend in the number of applicants and a decline in external funding.

First, the institution decides to maintain the admission standard. The simulated results of this policy are shown in Figure 5. Since the number of applicants decreases, the number of enrollees also decreases, from 10,000 in year 1 to 8187 by the end of year 10. The cost of tuition increases after year 4, and the per-student expenditure decreases negligibly. The institution's revenues decrease because of the assumption that non-

Figure 3. Flow Diagram of Institutional Revenue Sector

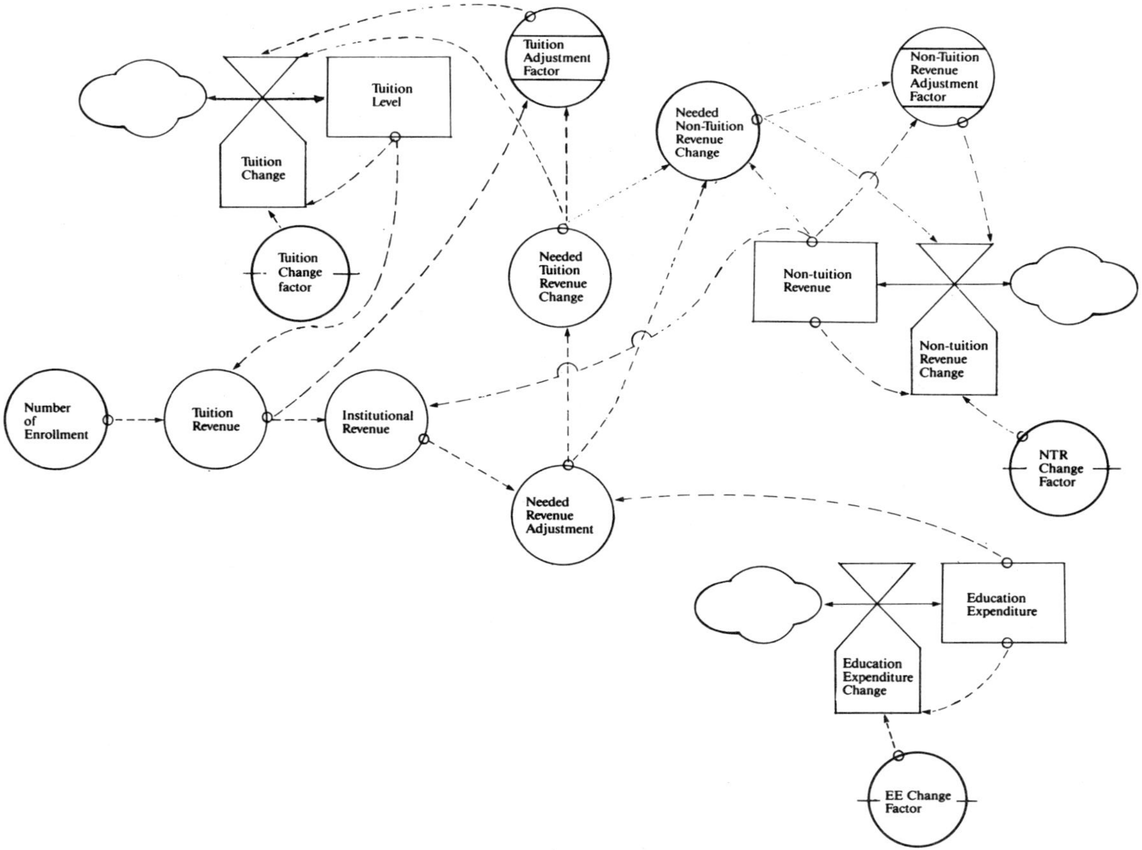

Tuition Adjustment Factor
Tuition Level
Tuition Change
Tuition Change factor
Needed Tuition Revenue Change
Needed Non-Tuition Revenue Change
Non-Tuition Revenue Adjustment Factor
Non-tuition Revenue
Non-tuition Revenue Change
NTR Change Factor
Number of Enrollment
Tuition Revenue
Institutional Revenue
Needed Revenue Adjustment
Education Expenditure
Education Expenditure Change
EE Change Factor

Figure 4. Scenario Testing of Applicant Increase

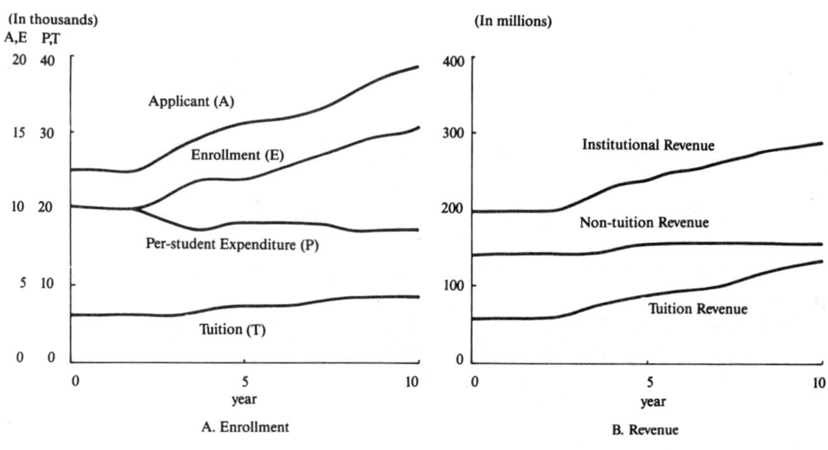

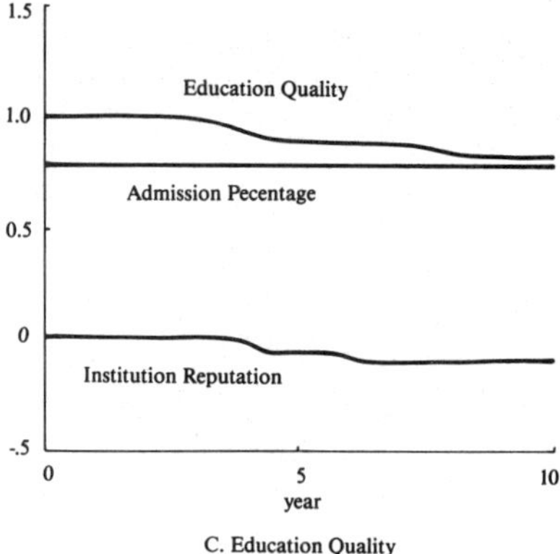

tuition revenue decreases and because tuition revenue remains the same. As shown in Graph B of Figure 5, under a constant admission standard the quality of education and the institutional reputation remain at essentially the same level. They fall only slightly after several years.

Figure 6 illustrates the model's behavior under a second policy: maintaining the enrollment level. It is assumed that the number of applicants declines. The number of enrollees remains at a steady level for about seven years and then sharply decreases. At the end of ten years, the enrollment decreases to 8220, almost the same as under the policy of maintaining the admission standard. The number of applicants, however, is about 2000 less than under the previous policy at the tenth year. This difference occurs because the admission standard must be lowered in order to maintain the level of enrollment, and a lower admission standard causes the quality of education and the institution's reputation to suffer. As the reputation declines, the number of applicants falls.

Tuition increases by about 22 percent by the end of the tenth year. This increase is about 7 percent higher than under the policy of maintaining the admission standard. By the fifth year, the per-student expenditure has dropped about $1400, or 7 percent. At the end of 10 years, however, the expenditure returns to the original level.

To summarize the differences between the two policies, the "steady enrollment" policy keeps enrollment relatively constant for a longer period of time, but by the end of the tenth year the two policies result in a comparable number of enrollees. The "steady enrollment" policy also results in far fewer applicants, a higher tuition level, a more dramatic change in the per-pupil expenditure level, and a noticeable decline in educational quality.

These differences are brought about because a policy of maintaining the same level of enrollment while the institution experiences a reduction in non-tuition revenues puts pressure on the institution to increase its tuition level. The combination of the lower admission standard and the reduction in the per-pupil educational expenditure has an adverse effect on the quality of education. In the long run, the reputation of the institution suffers, and even fewer applicants are attracted.

Future Model Development and Its Use in Policy Making

This study illustrates how the technique of system dynamics can be used to support decision making in higher education. Since this performance model is only illustrative, the uniqueness of the relationships among its assumptions must be stressed. When applied to a particular institutional setting, the assumptions would need to be tailored to other specific circumstances.

Generally speaking, there are three ways to modify and develop the

Figure 5. Policy Results of Maintaining the Admission Standard

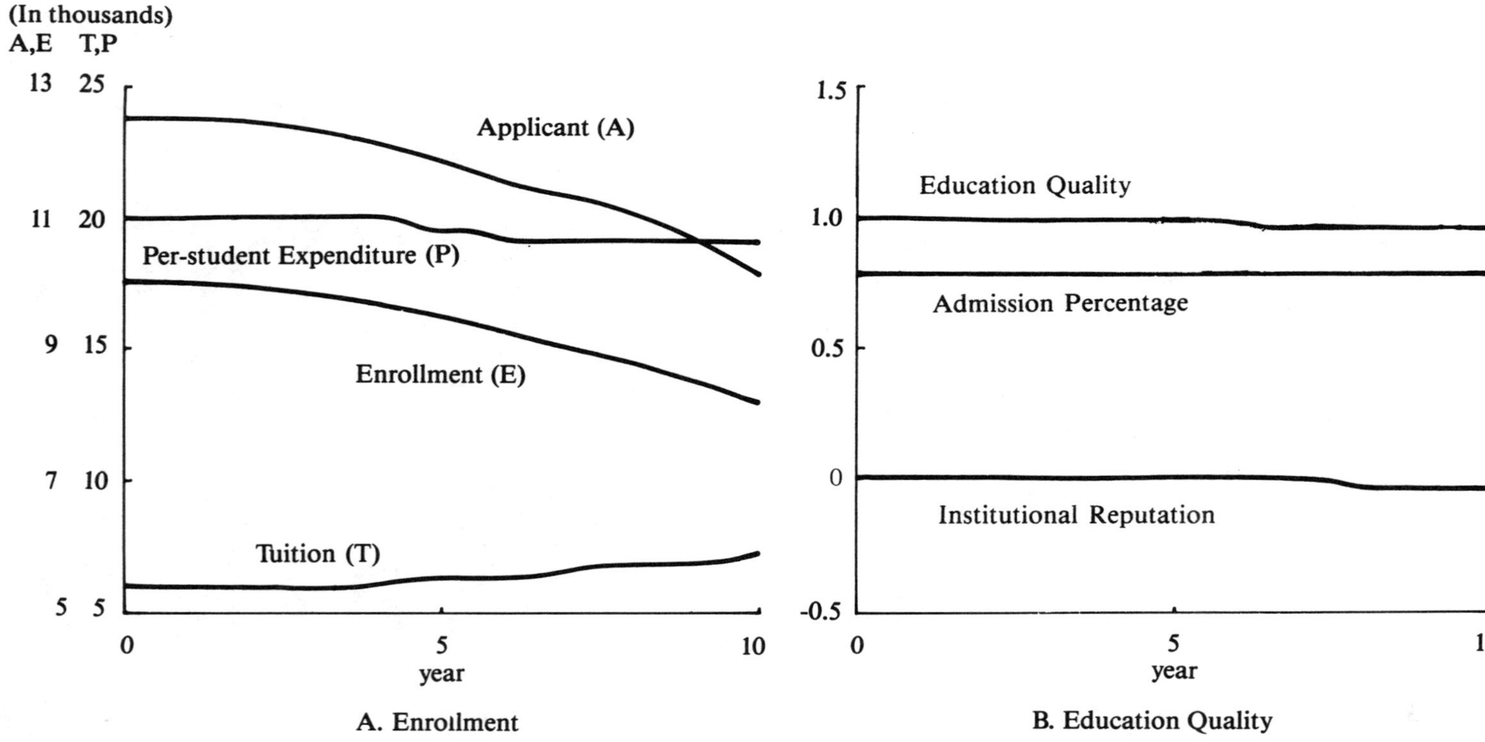

Figure 6. Policy Results of Maintaining the Enrollment Level

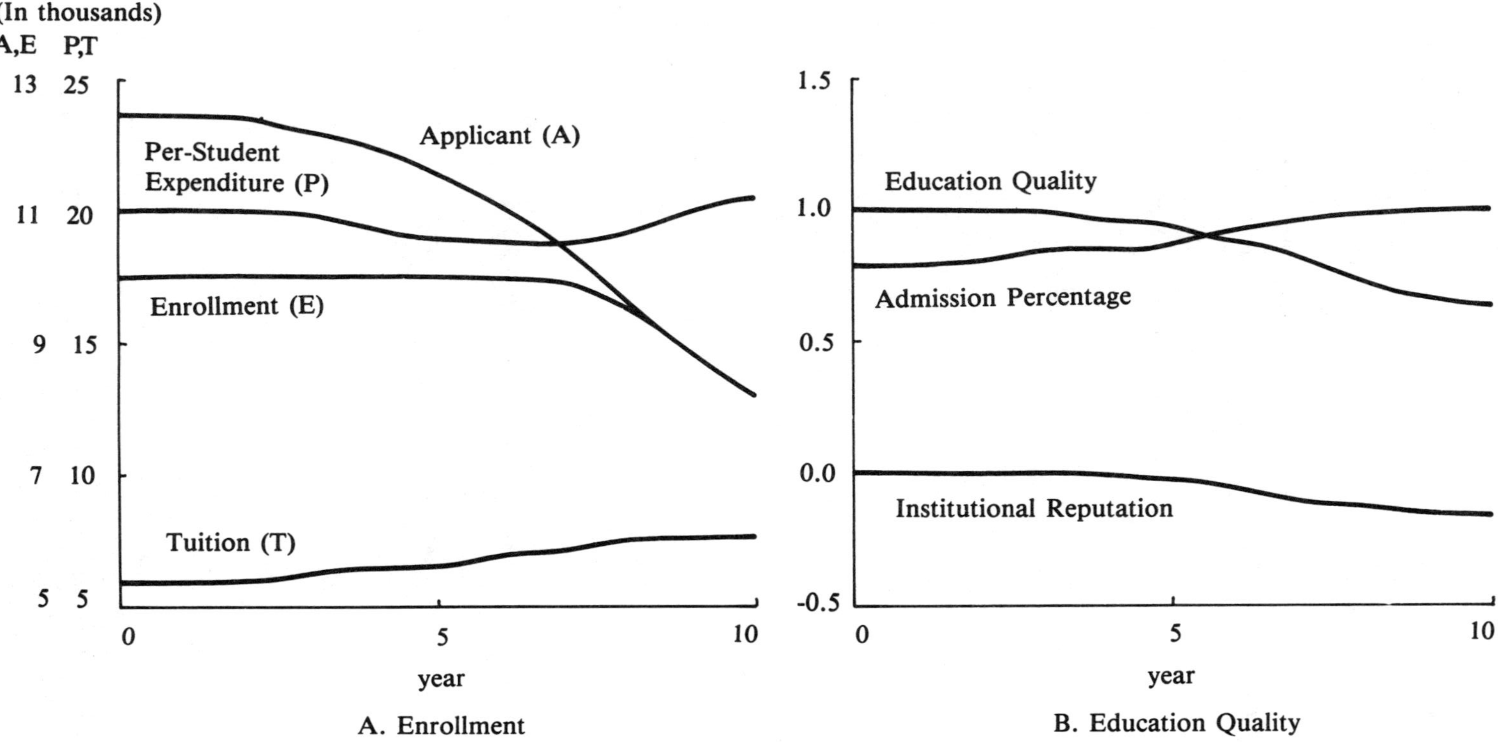

A. Enrollment

B. Education Quality

model: 1) changing the model parameters, 2) changing the model structure, and 3) changing the system boundary. Changing the model parameters, for example, might involve making non-tuition revenue more easily adjusted by the institution. An example of changing the model structure would be differentiating institutional support for education into support for staff/faculty and support for the campus facilities. Similarly, the relationship between the staff/faculty workload and morale could be analyzed. This model could also be extended to explore the relationship between the changes in tuition and the availability of financial aid (Karol and Ginsburg, 1980, p. 49). Finally, the system boundary could be enlarged or reduced. Some model builders might prefer to incorporate the dynamics of external revenues into the system. Others might find it useful to adapt system dynamics to the analysis of a smaller unit within the institution, such as a college or department. For readers who would like more information on building system dynamics models, Richardson and Pugh (1981) and Roberts and others (1983) provide introductions to the technique and its application.

References

Karol, N. H., and Ginsburg, S. G. *Managing the Higher Education Enterprise.* New York: Wiley, 1980.

Litten, L. H. (Ed.). *Issues in Pricing Undergraduate Education.* New Directions for Institutional Research, no. 42. San Francisco: Jossey-Bass, 1984.

Richardson, G. P., and Pugh, A. L., III. *Introduction to System Dynamics Modeling with DYNAMO.* Cambridge, Mass.: M.I.T. Press, 1981.

Roberts, E. N. "System Dynamics—An Introduction." In E. N. Roberts (Ed.), *Managerial Applications of System Dynamics.* Cambridge, Mass.: M.I.T. Press, 1978.

Roberts, N., Andersen, D., Deal, R., Garet, M., and Shaffer, W. *Introduction to Computer Simulation: A System Dynamics Modeling Approach.* Reading, Mass.: Addison-Wesley, 1983.

Turcotte, R. B. "Enrollment Management at the Graduate Level." *Journal of College Admissions,* 1983, *27* (4), 24–28.

Whitla, D. "The Admission Equation." *Change,* 1984, *16* (8), 20–30.

Fiona Chen has served as an assistant professor in public administration at Eastern Washington University from 1983 to 1985 and will be joining the public administration faculty at Florida State University in the fall of 1986.

Part 4.

Conclusion

Decision Support Systems need not be expansive or expensive in order to be effective in institutional settings.

The Future of Decision Support Systems in Institutional Research

John Rohrbaugh

Institutional problems such as workforce reductions, tenure decisions, budget allocations, and pricing are inherently complex and demand difficult choices. The act of deciding "what to decide" in instances such as these constitutes much of the challenge associated with administrative responsibility. It is in the continual demand for choice after choice, however, that more fundamental—and often more crucial—decisions are made repeatedly by default: deciding "how to decide."

The act of deciding how to decide assumes that there are well-understood alternative approaches to making a particular choice. Which of a variety of procedures or methods of decision making is appropriate in a given instance? The unfortunate fact seems to be that most individuals have far more clearly differentiated conceptions of alternative tennis serves or alternative golf swings than of alternative approaches to making a decision. For this reason, the act of deciding how to decide is only rarely an explicit, conscious process, in which one of many possible alternative approaches is selected with attention to its suitability for a given configuration of circumstances.

In fact, most individuals are unable to describe clearly and fully

J. Rohrbaugh, A. T. McCartt (Eds.). *Applying Decision Support Systems in Higher Education.* New Directions for Institutional Research, no. 49. San Francisco: Jossey-Bass, March 1986.

even one set of cognitive techniques or mental mechanisms by which they made a particular choice. Far better explanations are usually given of "how I serve a tennis ball" or "how I drive a golf ball" than of "how I made the decision." (Extensive descriptions of "how I collected information" are often provided, but that is not the question asked.) The ability to observe critically one's own decision-making behavior, the capacity for cognitive self-reflection, is as much a prerequisite for increasing the effectiveness of decision making as attention to one's body movements is a prerequisite for improving one's performance in tennis or golf.

The realization that there are many alternative approaches to making decisions and recognition of the strengths and weaknesses of each method lead to more explicit and conscious choices about how to decide. There appears to be an increasing awareness that the characteristics of a particular problem do not beget a single, right, and proper mechanism for its solution. Decision processes are selected because of the nature of decision makers rather than because of the nature of problems. Eden and others (1983) have emphasized that "problems are psychological entities which are often unclear and expressed as anxiety and concern about a situation as well as being expressed as a positive wish for the situation to be different. Problems are idiosyncratic constructions that belong to individuals" (p. x).

The importance of this emphasis on the subjective interpretation of institutional problems is that it throws open to question a simple one-to-one correspondence between an obvious problem type and a specific solution principle. A variety of approaches are available for the solution of any problem; therefore, the act of deciding how to decide is a critical one, indeed. The section that follows suggests one way in which alternative decision processes can be understood.

Evaluating Alternative Decision Processes

Quinn and others (1985) have suggested that alternative decision processes are evaluated from four perspectives: empirical, rational, political, and consensual. Each perspective employs unique assessment criteria that reflect particular institutional values. Depending upon the dominant perspective among decision makers, decisions about how to decide will be made in predictable ways.

The Empirical Perspective. This viewpoint emphasizes the importance of evidence in a decision process. Particular attention is directed to securing relevant information and developing large databases. Proponents of this perspective believe that to be effective, a decision process must allow thorough documentation and considerable accountability.

The Rational Perspective. Logic rather than data dominates this viewpoint, since clear thinking is seen as the primary ingredient for effective decision making. The process should be based on explicit attention to institutional goals and objectives. Methods that assist decision makers with their reasoning are particularly valued.

The Political Perspective. Nothing is viewed as more useful to decision making than the power resources that can accrue from a good idea. As a result, this perspective stresses the need for adaptability and flexibility in creative problem solving, while recognizing that final decisions must be seen as legitimate by other affected parties and responsive to shifts in uncertain and turbulent environments.

The Consensual Perspective. The most important assessment criterion in this perspective is the availability of a participatory process that allows open expression of individual feelings and sentiments. Internal discussion and debate are thought to lead to collective agreement on a mutually satisfactory solution. As a result, the likelihood of support for the decision during implementation is increased.

Choosing Among Perspectives

A common institutional problem such as office space assignments might be approached from any of these four perspectives. The empirical perspective might favor the development of space use inventories, office request forms, and surveys of student traffic patterns through corridors and doorways. The rational perspective might favor the design of multiattribute utility models, providing alternative assignments for each office with consideration of competing objectives for the use of campus space in accordance with institutional planning. The political perspective might favor proceeding informally, with a series of telephone calls, lunch conversations, and hallway discussions, to maintain plenty of administrative discretion over resources while final checks are made with one or two vice presidents and campus security. The consensual perspective might favor setting aside a day for the open discussion of office assignment problems and possibilities, during which all individuals directly affected by the outcome might have an extended opportunity to express their concerns. In all likelihood, the subjective interpretation of the institutional problem would vary considerably in these four hypothetical cases. The problem might eventually come to be seen as simple or complex, structured or unstructured, programmable or nonprogrammable, strategic or tactical.

Despite their differing approaches, all four perspectives appear to set reasonable standards for assessing decision processes. No single perspective is inherently all right or all wrong. This can be seen more easily when the perspectives are divided into four quadrants, as shown in Figure 1. The two axes suggest that the two perspectives toward the right (political and rational) are more externally focused, use less information, operate at greater speed, and are more concerned with impact, whereas the two perspectives toward the left (consensual and empirical) are more internally focused, use more information, operate more slowly, and are more concerned with process. The two perspectives toward the top (consensual and political) are more flexible, intuitive, implicit, and collectivized, whereas the two perspectives toward the bottom (empirical and rational) are more regulated, analytical, explict, and individualized. It is this latter distinction in perspectives that most dramatically differentiates two widely practiced approaches to decision support: the "hard" management science or operations research approach (empirical and rational) and the "soft" group process or organization development approach (political and consensual).

As Michael McGrath noted in Chapter 5, the development of DSS over the past 15 years has extended beyond "exhaustive" empiricism and "bounded" rationality to incorporate political and consensual perspectives as well. Unlike transaction systems or traditional reporting systems, DSS currently are built to provide considerable adaptability in design and architecture that readily permits iterative modifications and a phased approach approach to implementation. Not only are decision makers encouraged to confront problems in a flexible, personal manner, but, ideally, each DSS application can conveniently undergo changes to handle different or expanded sets of problems in alternative ways. With the advent of GDSS, decision support is now available for executive teams who wish to work collectively, exchange ideas, and move toward consensus on preferred courses of action. The role of decision support in participatory decision processes is an issue that will be explored extensively in the next ten years.

Institutional Effectiveness and Decision Support

Associated with each of the four perspectives are implicit beliefs about the best ways to assure successful DSS implementation, as well as the performance outcomes that are most important to achieve. According to Quinn and Rohrbaugh (1981, 1983), these four views of organizational effectiveness can be represented in juxtaposition, as shown in Figure 2. The internal process model of organizational effectiveness places great emphasis on control and internal focus. It stresses the role of information management and communication (as means) and stability and control (as ends) to achieve effectiveness in an institution. The rational goal model places great emphasis on control and external focus. It stresses the role of planning and goal setting (as means) and productivity and efficiency (as ends). The open system model places great emphasis on external focus and flexibility; it stresses the role of adaptability and readiness (as means) and resource acquisition and institutional growth (as ends). Finally, the human relations model places great emphasis on flexibility and internal focus and stresses the role of cohesion and morale (as means) and the enrichment of human resources (as an end). What suggestions for DSS implementation and evaluation derive from each model?

Figure 1. Four Perspectives for Evaluating Decisions

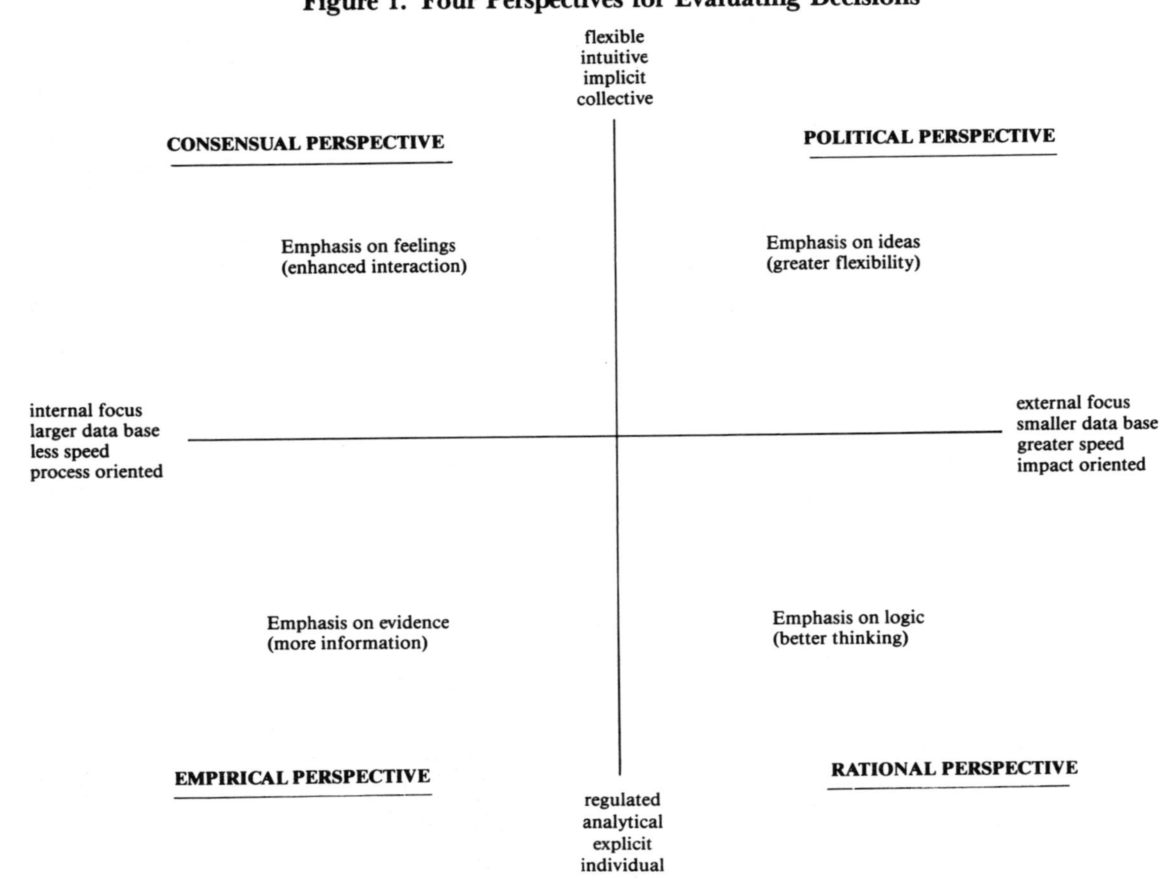

Figure 2. Four Models of Organizational Effectiveness

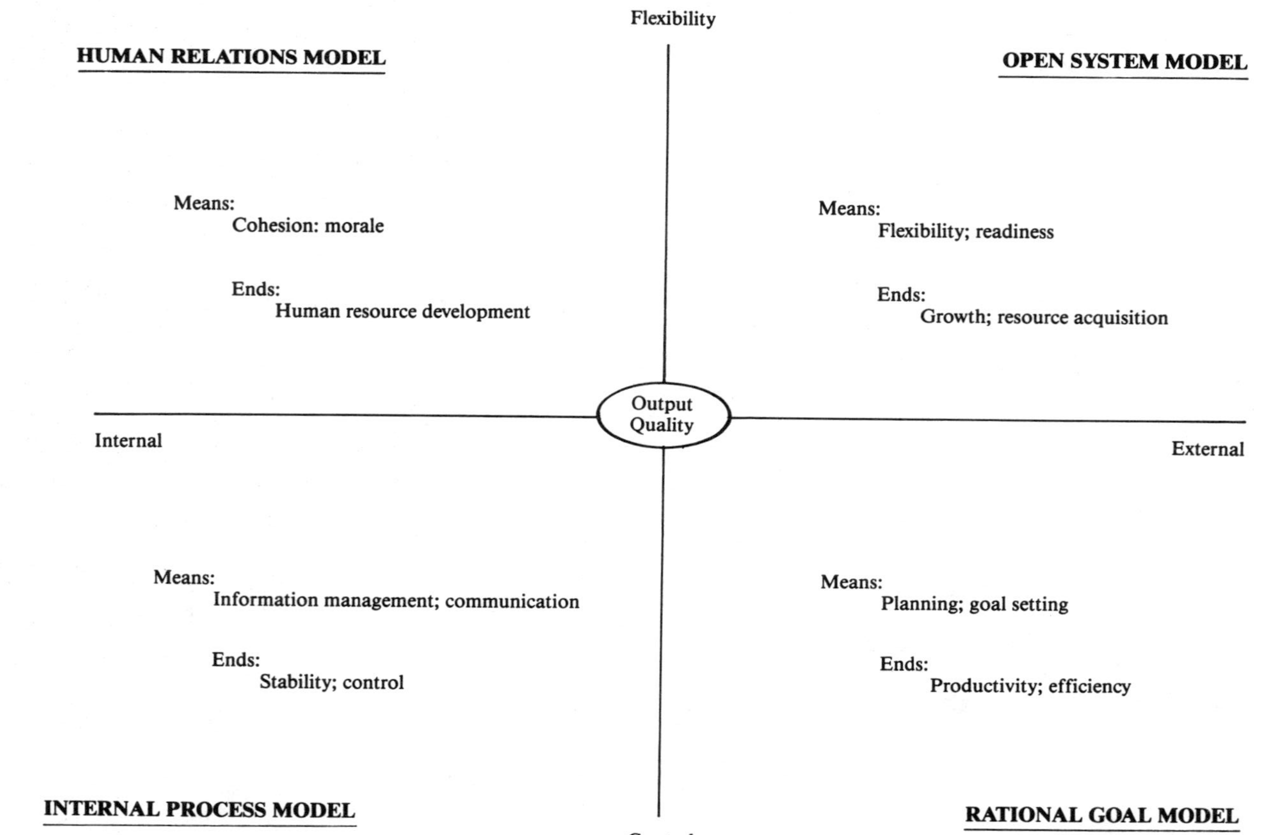

The Internal Process Model. Early efforts to develop DSS applications should minimize the amount of institutional change demanded, so as to assure continuity and facilitate coordination. Existing data bases and report formats might well be maintained and used. The DSS design does not need to be expansive; in fact, simple systems with simple outputs are usually easier to understand, implement, and modify. Even if the problem is thought to demand complexity in the design, the decision support provided does not need to restrict user comprehension. In short, the main concerns here are respecting existing organizational control and stability and minimizing the threat of innovation.

The Rational Goal Model. Under this approach, extensive preparation and planning are essential to the accomplishment of the institutional objectives set for the use of DSS. Among the risks associated with implementation that need to be anticipated are unwilling users, multiple implementers, disappearing maintainers, vague purpose or poorly specified usage pattern, inability to predict impact, loss or lack of support, inexperience with such systems, and unanticipated costs (Keen and Scott Morton, 1978). This view would favor design of an inexpensive prototype, particularly when the proposed application is particularly innovative for the institution. Success with the prototype might lead to additional investment and development, but the initial experience and understanding are gained at relatively small cost.

The Open System Model. The design of DSS must be an adaptable process leading to a flexible system of decision support. Most systems are developed through a gradual, evolutionary approach that permits tailoring to meet the changing needs of individual decision makers and executive teams. Unlike the internal process view, this model stresses the virtues of innovation and adjustment as opposed to institutional continuity and stability. Users and builders alike will need to understand DSS applications as ongoing services rather than as finished products. Because this model is most concerned with the acquisition of power resources and institutional development, opportunities should be sought to increase awareness. An existing system can be expanded, tackling new problems or designing additional prototypes.

The Human Relations Model. This sourcebook has stressed the critical importance of user participation in every phase of development. Participation not only increases the likelihood that a system will be used; it also reduces the probability of major flaws in design. Institutional resources must be made available to support adequate training of users. Their skills must be enhanced so they can benefit from decision support and contribute to subsequent development initiatives. The requisite resources include readily available hardware and software, technical staff time, and—most important—a clear commitment from the decision makers that their interest and attention will not be deflected to other pressing institutional problems. An effective project to develop DSS capabilities should contribute significantly to enriching the human resources of the institution.

The Future of Decision Support Systems

All four models (internal process, rational goal, open system, and human relations) make significant contributions to a full understanding of effective decision support. In combination, they lead to an appreciation that future institutional concerns must be directed both internally and externally, both at maintaining control and increasing flexibility, at improving both performance outcomes and the processes that produce them. Attempts to accommodate these competing expectations for institutional performance can produce severe organizational tensions. Nevertheless, no effort involving institutional change can avoid coming to terms with these dilemmas of leadership (Quinn and Rohrbaugh, 1983).

The design and implementation of DSS can allow an institution to become more effective in many areas: information management, resource acquisition, efficiency, cohesion, flexibility, productivity, human resource development, and stability. It is interesting to note that attention to all of these concerns also leads to effective design and implementation of DSS. Although the fifteen-year history of DSS (as well as the much longer history of organization theory) has been dominated by narrow vantage points, the profession of institutional research demands an all-encompassing paradigm. No one perspective on organizational decision making, nor any one model of organizational effectiveness, is sufficient. In the future, institutional decision making will be well supported when system design fully incorporates empirical, rational, political, and consensual interests.

References

Eden, C., Jones, S., and Sims, D. *Messing About in Problems: An Informal Structured Approach to Their Identification and Management.* New York: Pergamon, 1983.

Keen, P. G. W., and Scott Morton, M. S. *Decision Support Systems: An Organizational Perspective.* Reading, Mass.: Addison-Wesley, 1978.

Quinn, R. E., and Rohrbaugh, J. "A Competing Values Approach to Organizational Effectiveness." *Public Productivity Review,* 1981, *5,* 122–140.

Quinn, R. E., and Rohrbaugh, J. "A Spatial Model of Effectiveness Criteria: Towards a Competing Values Approach to Organizational Analysis." *Management Science,* 1983, *29,* 363–377.

Quinn, R. E., and Rohrbaugh, J., and McGrath, M. R. "Automated Decision Conferencing: How It Works." *Personnel,* 1985, *21,* 49–55.

John Rohrbaugh is associate professor in the Rockefeller College of Public Affairs and Policy, State University of New York at Albany.

Index

E

F

G

H

I

J

K

Q

R

S

T

U

V

W

Y

Z